THE SPACE BETWEEN

How to Wait on God When
You Would Rather Not

Keep the faith —
All things
work for the
good!

SARA CONNER

Love

Bulk orders can be obtained by contacting **www.pastorsara.com**

The Space Between

ISBN-13: 978-0-9996027-1-3

www.pastorsara.com

Thanks

Eben, Heaven and Landon my USA home team, my Jamaican crew – Tommy (Dad), Carlene, my siblings, Che, Shikisha, Saidah, Nathan, and Naomi. Vincent and Mishondia Robinson for helping me out. Monita & Gabi for hours of labor. Word of Truth; I am better at this stuff now because of you.

Wait on the LORD: be of good courage, and he shall strengthen thine heart: wait, I say, on the LORD. Psalm 27:14

.

.

.

But

I

Don't

Want

To

Table of Contents:

Introduction: **Bare Those Bones**

Let me just lay it bare right here. I am no stranger to disappointment and strongly suspect you are not either. Each day, as sure as a mountain has a peak or the east welcomes a sunrise, we are all guaranteed an audience with disappointment. As it rears its head in a life event, a broken promise, a personal letdown, or an unmet expectation; disappointment challenges us to engage in a fight for our faith.

Disappointment has gripped its cold wobbly fingers around various seasons of my life; its touch left me disappointed in myself, others, and I sheepishly say, in God. When the unexpected happens and my plans fail, I become impatient, miserable, and irritable, moving swiftly into the "woe is me, my life is horrendous" state of mind that has me doubting who God is and who I am to Him.

Tired of living this yo-yo life between faith and doubt, I decided to make a change. Grabbing a notebook and a pen, I took the journey of tracking the moments of disappointment. Those moments when I wanted to resign. By turning over these rocks and paying attention to the times I wanted to give up, something interesting revealed itself in my life: Thoughts of caving in usually came during times of transition and stress.

Some of these moments were easy to pinpoint. Getting married and moving to a new country without any family was an opportunity to be disappointed in myself, since I had assumed I would catch on to the American culture quicker than I did. In 1998, my husband was injured in a car accident and lost the ability to physically provide for us in the same manner as he had before. Once again, an opportunity for stress and disappointment.

There have also been moments when my faith succumbed to my situation but at the time I didn't recognize what all was occurring. I live in the countryside of Mansfield, Texas. One evening, while driving on a dark, winding road, I could barely see 10 feet in front of me due to a thick, blinding fog. My headlights were of little help. Suddenly, an image appeared in the dense fog. I noticed that I was about to collide with an object in the road. Swerving to the left and pressing my brakes to the floor my car came to a labored stop. Shocked and completely undone, my heart raced wildly. I looked in front of the car to see the backside of a horse facing me. It was a collision I was unprepared for. Was I going too fast to see the signs? Was I not paying attention? Was I distracted? Or had I just lost focus?

Some seasons in my faith journey have been just like that experience. The disappointment hit my heart suddenly; the stress snuck up on me. I panicked, reacted, and in trying to avoid dealing with it, I barely escaped. Or, in some cases, I had a head-on collision.

It seemed to me this emotional response didn't happen at the beginning of the journey. I was most excited at the beginning. It didn't happen at the end either because I finally saw what I was hoping for materialize. I could celebrate then. A lot of my discouragement happened while I was waiting on something to happen.

The Wait

While waiting on God to bring to pass a promise, a vision, a dream, or a plan – something I thought should have already materialized – I get stuck, sidetracked, distracted, deceived, frustrated, angry, and isolated. At that point, I give up. The fog of emotions I find myself in raises this question in my heart: "God, I know you have promises for me, but why are they taking so long to come to pass?"

Have you ever asked that question? I am sure you have! Some of us (myself included) even add questions like: "How is Sally Sue Jones getting her promise and mine is on backorder?" or "Lord, Where are You?" and "Lord, Are You even listening?"

Freedom. I needed to be free from this cycle of frustration and anger. Believing God one minute and doubting him seconds later. Once I pinpointed I was squandering my victories during the space between, I made up my mind. I needed to figure out how to stop flunking and start winning in all seasons of my life. Especially in the space between moments of my journey.

Between

Between. This word describes the times of waiting in my life. Most of my meltdowns and build-ups loom in the "meantime" stages of my life. There is always a gap between the image I have of my dream and where I am currently. That gap denotes the hyphen in life that signifies the middle portion of the process. I am most susceptible to disappointment during these between seasons of my life. I often entertain the thought that God must have forgotten to check His calendar, for surely I am due a blessing. There in those between places I am severely tempted to give up and give in, to abandon ship, or to simply check out.

I am a Christian. I believe in God and His power, but truth be told, I do not always want to wait on His good and perfect timing. I want to just think a thing and, like I Love Genie, nod my head, wiggle my nose, and with lightning speed have my promise appear. However, I find that this process does not quite work the way I want it to. In fact, this process often makes me want to pull my hair out instead of fall to my knees in prayer.

I walked through several betweens in my life, and I made a royal mess of some of them. But I believe God taught me some things through His Word while on those journeys. These pages intend to reveal those learned lessons so you can avoid some of the pitfalls on the path to receiving your promised dream from God. If you are not careful, the between space of waiting can become a valley of dried bones sucking life out of your destiny instead of segueing you into your next moment of triumph.

By the end of our time together, I hope to have brought some encouragement, understanding, support, and relief to you while you are in the waiting room of your promise. I included questions to jog your heart and jumpstart your internal travels. Some of these questions will bring a smile to your face, while others may make you cringe. But really, how honest is self-reflection without a cringe or two?

Will you be courageous and join me on this journey? Do not worry, we will get to the part where we kick up our heels, blow bubbles, and celebrate. In the meantime, we may cry some, stomp some, and cover our ears some, but together we will go through, and together you and I will learn how to win while we WAIT.

Go ahead and get comfortable. Grab your blanket, get on your favorite couch, stock up on chocolates for me and carrot sticks for you. Grab a pen and some cool highlighters. Get cozy, practice saying, "Amen, sister, Amen!" and let's dig in.

Let Us Pray

Father God, we come to You asking Your Holy Spirit to illuminate our hearts as we learn from Your Word about how good You are, how faithful to Your promises You remain, and how to navigate the between seasons of our lives. Use these pages to birth faith in our hearts like never before as we continue trusting You to manifest Your will in our lives. In Jesus' Name, Amen.

One

The Space Between

It is really awkward now. I am very annoyed. Piercing her with my "you are getting on my nerves" stare, I expect a reaction, but she is oblivious to it. She hardly even notices me. It is hard to believe she is totally ignorant of the fire-breathing dragon behind her. Into the endless folds of vinyl, her forearm disappears. My ears ring from the annoying sound of loose coins hitting each other between her fingers.

The clicking of the change grates my ears and my foot begins to tap to the incessant, haphazard rhythm. "Lady, hurry up already." My thoughts are so loud that I look around to see if anyone else hears them. I want her to hear. My impatience seethes now and I am not sure why the shifting of my weight from side to side, the folding of my arms, heavy breathing, and mumblings beneath my breath all go unnoticed. I scream inside and literally throw a fit, albeit internally. "Let's get on with it already. Hey lady, let's move it."

She asks the cashier to break a twenty because she does not have the change she had been searching for, in slow motion. I am about to explode. It seems like a millennium has passed since she started rustling through her pockets. I have had it. I cannot and will not wait anymore. I have to go. This is a huge waste of my time. I should just pay for her stuff. The more hostile I become, the slower she gets, as if in retribution for my anger. She is like a turtle doing tai chi, moseying on with what I am certain is a lullaby playing in her blessed head. I give up. I resign. I may be stuck in a retail nightmare for the next day or two if I do nothing but wait. I cave. My shoulders slump. I am bored and inattentive. I wish somebody had told me that getting a baby outfit would take this much time. I literally spend more time trying to check out than I did picking the outfit.

I am resentful and wonder if I should even stay in this line. I gripe and belittle myself to pass the time. Surely there was another option and I was just too dumb to see it. A dark cloud of gloom hangs over my head as I banter, "You mean Christian girl. Why are you frustrated with the elderly woman who cannot find her change?" I start to negotiate with myself.

"I can wait, can't I?"

"Just do this another time."

"Sara, do you want to pay this lady's bill right now?"

"Is there somewhere else I can get this done faster?"

"Shoot. Is it really worth this wait?"

Finally, I decide. You know what? I will leave the baby outfit here. When I have more time I will come back and get it. Oh man. I am so deflated now. As I walk away, I look back and see that the lady in front of me finally finished. This makes me doubly mad at myself. I do not have my item. I wasted minutes I'll never get back. I was irritated the entire time, and now I do not even feel like going to the baby shower. The simple task of grabbing a gift turned into an emotional ordeal that threatened to steal the joy out of the party I was to attend, and all because I did not plan in advance. By rushing, I expected everything else and everyone around me to speed up. I did not want to wait but honey, I wanted to be waited on. It would have been better in my mind if everything went according to my plan. As a matter of fact, if the cashier could have read my mind, had the outfit at the counter, locked the store and waited for me to bring my glorious self there, then we would have had a perfect ending. But that's not realistic to think I can get what I want, when I want, without any effort on my part, while the universe rotates on its axis around my desires. Sounds utterly ridiculous. Yet, that is exactly what we are doing when we want to get the end result without the work required.

Everyone wants the promise, but few are willing to endure the process. Excruciating, is it not? The Wait – the suspended period of time between what we want and when we get it. Waiting is the extractor of our patience and the judge of our endurance. It comes cloaked in a simple word named "and." This three-letter word is way bigger than it lets on. Small but significant, this word is the link that connects the beginning of a journey to its end. It spans the breadth of time from the moment I pray for something and when I see it actualize. It is the range between here and there. It is the distance from initiating my sacrifice and the moment I see success. It is the dash that separates my past and my future. Waiting is the interval that holds my dreams captive while I walk out the maturation process needed to achieve them.

We should ask ourselves this question: "Is the thing I am believing God for worth the wait?" While we toss around the pros and cons, the ifs and buts, the could-haves and should-haves, we run the risk of losing sight of the fact that

> the in-between process can actually be the single most important factor in getting what we desire.

Why? Because we cannot avoid it.

Meltdowns in the Middle

It is during the in-between times that we either lose faith and abandon hope, or we surrender, learn, and grow. Many dreams are sabotaged during the pilgrimage of waiting. During this season, the storms of life batter and assail our callings, urging them to bow or stand strong. Piece by piece we see them tossed by the winds of betrayal, disappointment, frustration, impatience, arrogance, indifference, and misdirection.

It is in the waiting period that a cake collapses if pulled out before its time. It is there that a plant surrenders its last breath if uprooted prematurely. Sadly, it is also in the waiting that believers often collapse in their faith, grasping for threads, reaching for an assurance it will all work out in the end. The space between can be excruciating or it can be wonderful. What it cannot be is ignored, skipped over or prayed away. It can only be walked through.

I have been in the belly of the wait many times. I wish I could tell you it has all gone well, that I have been steadfast in my faith and immoveable in my resolve. I could play the saint and pretend I have walked on water and done enough holy hops to skip this part of the process. But the reality is, my life is the same as yours, and the most proven and perfect way to get through the "and" is actually to wait. Sounds too basic. I know. This concept is really not complicated. However, in true Sara fashion, I always envision a perfect way of getting through it. Maybe you are like me and have a preconceived idea of how something is supposed to go once you dream it, picture it, imagine it, or desire it.

I mean, it is simple, right? In my mind I do not see any reason to wait. I should just be able to have a dream and bam! Shazaam! It quickly appears. With wind in my hair and a spring in my step, I should arrive at my destination in life, filtered and blemish-free. All the while fans will scream my name and English chocolates will fill my pockets. Yes.

That is how I would get through The Wait. Like a playwright or the director of a film, I prefer to edit out the parts I do not like. If given the opportunity, I would more than likely erase from the storyboard the pieces that irritate me and assign everyone in the cast a part to play in fulfilling my vision.

Ok, judge me if you want, but the inner me is allergic to pain. I naturally avoid the hard and disappear from the difficult. Meanwhile, I relish the easy. I embrace quick methods and I absolutely love being comfortable. But here are the cold-hard facts: having seen the process of a promise play out over and over in my own life, I learned that

> that "easy" does not create exceptional results and "quick" does not qualify you to receive the promises God has declared over your life.

The fact is, I noticed time and time again that it is usually the slow and not the sudden that God uses to bring forth the supernatural in our lives. I always hope that things will happen quickly, but I found it is the discipline that waiting brings which creates the foundation on which my calling can be built. In fact, more is accomplished in shorter time-periods when I actually "let patience have its perfect work…" (James 1:4a, NKJV) than when I resist the change God wants to do in my heart on my way to obtaining whatever promise I am believing Him to fulfil.

We are not alone in this process of life. Many people before us paved the way for us to observe and follow. Through their lives we gain warning signs and winning strategies that can bring hope to our own situations.

Clouded Maps

Allow me to engage your imagination for a moment as we journey back to the birth of the nation of Israel. There was a time when this great nation did not exist, but God chose one man, and made him a promise:

> "Now the Lord had said to Abram: Get out of your country, from your family and from your father's house, to a land that I will show you. I will make you a great nation; I will bless you and make your name great; and you shall be a blessing. I will bless those who bless you, and I will curse him who curses you; and in you all the families of the earth shall be blessed." Genesis 12:1-3, NKJV

Abram was the child of an idol worshipper, a trader of idols as the Talmud (a central text of Judaism) explains. However, one day he had an encounter with the Living God and chose to follow Him. When Abram was 75 years old, God spoke to him and gave him a grand and beautiful vision of his future. He used colorful words like "great nation," "bless you," "land," and "great name." God went so far as to say that all the families of the earth would be blessed because of Abram. Bringing to his imagination a promise of a child. How incredible is that? An amazing future was described. It really sounded as if everything was being set up in Abram's favor, organized for his benefit, and coordinated for his success.

I can imagine the joy Abram must have felt as he listened to God describe His marvelous plans for his success, fame, and prosperity. Honestly, if I were Abram, I would be a bit giddy. I would probably run outside and yell to my Bedouin neighbors to come celebrate with me. Roast the lamb! Break out the tambourine and kick up the desert sand with dancing feet! That is how I imagine it. Being the patriarch of the family God would choose to bless the entire earth through, must have sounded like the grandest idea since sliced bread. However, I am almost certain that while it all felt like a great honor, it was also terrifying. It makes me wonder if Abram spent time musing over all of the ramifications of the promise that would change his life forever. As he sat in the desert mulling this over, did he ever think that the desert would be more than a place he lived? That it could become a season in his life he would have to work through? I wonder.

God only revealed the destination in His conversation with Abram. He did not include anything about the journey. Many times it is the same for us. We latch onto the end product and skip over the "ands" placed strategically in between the promise of God and its actualization. I am sure Abram would never guess that desert living, enslavement, war, barrenness, name-change, and famine would be the "in-betweens" he and his family would have to endure on the way to realizing God's promise.

When God told Abram about the future, there was no mention of the fights or difficulties. There was no indication of the duration of the wait, the middle piece – the space between. The detail of Sarai being barren until her 90th birthday was not a headline of that discussion. That was twenty-five years after Abraham was first promised an heir. Abram's and Sarai's name change to Abraham and Sarah were omitted. Abraham lying with Hagar (Sarah's maid) and birthing an illegitimate son (Ishmael) did not make its way into the prophecy. The near sacrifice of his promised son, Isaac, just did not happen to come up in that defining conversation. All of these stops on the journey were embedded in the subtle conjunctions joining one idea to another. Each "and" became entire months, decades, even centuries of waiting wrapped up in a three-lettered pith.

> Waiting is the threshing floor of faith.

To wait is the ultimate litmus test of our grit. It is the 'coup de grace' of our stamina. We may want to avoid it, run from it, and resist it, but inside we know we must endure it. We must embrace the haunting necessity of the wait if we are to see the fulfillment of the promise.

I want to show you this is inescapable. The Bible let's us see a pattern. As with Abram, we see this process play out for another young man in the Bible…

Desert Dreams

Basking in the sun, the bronze melanin danced as golden flecks across his skin. His infectious laugh robust with confidence, caused his head to tilt to the left "just so" when he walked through the camp drawing the attention of all. Eyes glimmered every time his name echoed in the air revealing a bittersweet truth: he was different; he was favored. The firstborn son of Jacob's true love, Rachel, Joseph gallantly bore the reminder of that special bond. Joseph was a young teen when, God gave him a vision of his future. In a graphic dream, he saw his fate so clearly. He was destined to rule. His authority would be so great that even his brothers would bow down to him. Though he was not sure what it all meant, Joseph relished the dream. He was only seventeen years old when he received this picture of his promise (see Genesis 37:2-5), and he shared it with great excitement. However, the dream did not reveal that he would be sold as a slave, plotted against, persecuted, stalked, accused, forgotten and imprisoned. The timeline between the dream at seventeen and it coming to pass thirteen years later (see Genesis 41:46) was hidden in the process and not announced in the prophecy. I find that this rings true in our lives as well. We get to taste the sweetness of the future, but are a little in the dark regarding some of the bitter stops we must make on the way there. Like Joseph who ended up being blessed by God because he endured those bitter moments, we too can get better from the bitter.

Bitter Taste

My mom had a Chinese father born in Guangzhou, China, so we were fed on various interesting Chinese foods growing up: alien-looking lily roots, chewy octopus, dense cow tongue with hot mustard, dark dong quai soup for menstrual health, and airy lotus root, just to name a few. The one vegetable I did not like was that ugly, warty-textured, rough bitter melon. It was insipid. No matter how you sliced it, stir-fried it, parched it, or drowned it in oyster sauce, it just insisted on being harsh. I would eat it and my face could not control its contortions, wincing from the anticipated but underestimated tartness of the bitter melon. I hated it. However, even though I did not like it, I was forced to eat it. I was told, "It is good for your blood, and it will keep your immune system strong. Bitter is good for you." To avoid the rod of correction, I used the fork of ingestion, and begrudgingly ate the bitter melon. Waiting is just like that – at times bitter, but good for us, and though it is good for us, it can be ugly. If we are not careful, we also can become ugly within the waiting instead of becoming better through it.

Our heart begins to cry out its most sincere hopes in the waiting. Our need for God and His gentle touch become more evident. We ache for signs of His love, clues of His presence, and seek to find any footprints of His tenderness toward us.

> Waiting melts us, reducing us to who we really are: people in need of a faithful God.

We have to wait. Coming out on the other side is dependent on whether we will wait in our own strength or walk in the grace of God. Success is waiting on us to decide to bite the bit. Take the step into our promise understanding there is a space between. This space can break us or build us. We alone can make the choice on the route we want to take. The “Fall Apart” route or the “Faith in our Heart” route.

Falling apart is exactly what it means. We breakdown and allow our emotions to pull us away from the next step in moving forward. While the faith in our heart route is based on what we know over what we feel. Both routes are subject to our will. We get to decide the approach we will take.

Practical Application

This is it…the time for you to decide if you will submit to the process of the between or if you will circumvent your promise by refusing to take full part in the process. Throughout this book, I give you practical tools to help you do well while you wait. However, the decision is ultimately up to you whether (or not) you allow the waiting seasons to mold and shape you into the person you need to be. You can use the space below to begin journaling your journey.

Consider It

What is a promise you currently are waiting on to come to pass in your life?

Own my own business
Healthy relationships
Walk in my truth/purpose
Jesus Centered wife/husband relationship

How long have you been waiting?

1 year / 6 months

How have you approached seasons of waiting up until this point in your life? Do you think you need a new perspective? If yes, why?

Maybe. I remember when I waited for about 3-5 months on Graduate School.. during that time I prayed & didn't let negative stay for long.

Since, we cannot avoid waiting. How will you choose to begin waiting from today?

Learning about God more & trusting or activating/affirming my promises more. Focusing on what I need & letting the promises be held in the fathers hand. Knowing while I wait he is working. Trust Trust Trust. knowing how to trust myself.

Internalize It

Meditate on and memorize this scripture:

Now faith is the substance of things hoped for, the evidence of things not seen. Hebrews 11:1, NKJV

Speak It

"The Lord has given me a promise, and I will choose to believe it with a heart of faith until I see it come to pass. He will give me grace in the waiting. Grace to obey. Grace to have a good attitude. And Grace to see that I am being molded more into the image of Christ during the process of the in-between. I am well able to remain faithful and committed during this season."

Apply It

God has the very best in mind for your life. Take this scripture, put it on your mirror, and remind yourself of this promise every day:

"For I know the plans I have for you," says the Lord. "They are plans for good and not for disaster, to give you a future and a hope." Jeremiah 29:11, NLT

What does this verse show you about the heart of God?

It shows me that he is kind & loves me despite my flaws. That he knows me! Because to give me hope & a future means he knows what I need and what I want. It shows me he is a gentleman prepared & he cares about me when I always didn't put him first. It shows me his heart is HUGE full of hope, goodness, & love.

Imagine true love finding you. Living life and having someone witnessing your truth with an open heart. The joy of being showered with affection and the center of someone's awed attention. It is possible. The book of 1 Samuel lets us know about this kind of adoration enjoyed by a woman named Hannah. She was extremely treasured by her husband whose heart was set on making her happy. Hannah was a righteous young woman. From the outside, she looked beautiful. Her life appeared easy. She seemed to have it made. She was well taken

Two

Out of Breath

care of by the love of her life and her needs were met, but there was this inner longing that was wearing her down on the inside. Hannah had an ache in her heart that no gift, husband, wealth, nor position could satisfy. She was so consumed with this desire that no amount of words could describe the crippling effect it had on her heart. Where syllables failed, tears overflowed.

Hannah collapsed on the floor, her chest heaving with each jagged breath. Her gasps of despair began to make their final curtain call. The desperation of her longing soul reached out with frail arms, begging for hope to stay. Desperate wheezes mixed with tears burned with salt from her welted eyes as her wilted heart strained to gather the little faith she had left. Hannah wanted a child. As a young married woman with an adoring husband, childbirth should have been the next step in her carefully-crafted fairytale. But that step turned out to be steeped in disappointment. No matter her efforts, she could not produce a child. The desire for a baby had taken Hannah to despairing depths. It consumed her thoughts and controlled her life. Suffering in silence with a dream unfulfilled, the only solace she found was in the temple where she pled her case before God. She had done all she could. Her delirious crying and imbalance was such that Eli the priest mistook her for being drunk. Hannah was not crying in a cute fashion. It was a broken down, all or nothing, I-do not-care kind of crying.

In today's society, walking through the process of wanting a baby is not something you have to do alone. You can find support groups, fertility experts, counseling professionals, adoption agencies, and prayer warriors to beat down Heaven's door for you. Yet, in Hannah's culture and time, barrenness was an embarrassment. There is a morning blessing in the Jewish Talmud that highlights a perspective of women in those days. It states, "Blessed are you, Lord our God, ruler of the universe, who has not created me a woman." Imagine waking up to the chiming sounds of that if you were a woman back then. Women were measured by the number of sons they bore, and infertility was seen as a woman's affliction. Infertility could even provide grounds for a husband to divorce his wife, as barrenness was interpreted as disobedience to God's command to be fruitful and multiply. In cases like Hannah's, her husband had the right to divorce her or take an additional wife so that the commandment could be fulfilled.

Another aspect of childbearing in those days was the deep belief that God opened or closed wombs. Inability to bear a child was viewed as a sign that God's hand was against you and barrenness was evidence of His punishment (see Gen. 20:18). In essence, barrenness marked you as one who did not have the favor of God. Barrenness notified the community that you were less than, undeserving, and worthy only of abandonment.

It is in this scenario that we find Hannah desiring and waiting. Loved but lost. The stakes are high, and the wait is long. I will not assume to know exactly how long Hannah was barren, but I do know that the Mishnah, or oral law, provided a ten-year span for a woman to produce a child. After the ten years, a husband was free to divorce or add a wife. As a result of this law, I can assume that Hannah had been barren for a decade or more. Her husband had married a second wife named Penninah for the purpose of posterity. This wife became

Hannah's adversary. Hannah's worth, purpose, and sense of calling were on the brink of extermination if she did not produce children. This was a big deal!

Hannah was trapped between her unfulfilled desires and witnessing Penninah pop babies out like a rabbit. It was not fair. Her husband loved her incredibly, and yet his love was not enough to fill the longing in Hannah's heart. Her thoughts would run wild. Maybe she should just accept her fate and live in the shadows. Giving up had to have been a temptation. Broken yet bold, Hannah surrendered to her pain. She cried. She cried at home and she cried at church. She stopped eating and grief incapacitated her as she described herself this way: "I am a woman of sorrowful spirit." (1 Samuel 1:15, NKJV)

The name Hannah means "favored", but the wait began to take its toll on her. It felt like favor was nowhere in sight. The happy, treasured girl was now in the body of a woman cloaked in years of sadness. As the twisted hands of failure wrapped around her, Hannah became tethered to sorrow. Instead of changing for the better within, the wait changed her for the worse without. After more than ten years of waiting, she was so broken that she did the greatest injustice against herself by declaring failure instead of faith. She replaced the name of favor with a label called sorrow.

> The worst thing you can do in waiting on God; is speak death over yourself

You must resist the temptation no matter how you feel.

Living in a state of sorrow is not something that just happens; it is the result, over time, of the hope in your heart getting replaced by hopelessness. It took years for Hannah to get to this level of despair. Hannah had endured, season after season, of the other woman in the family consistently embarrassing her in an already shameful circumstance. Imagine for a moment seeing Penninah's enlarged belly, taut and filled with yet another new life. The women in the community place their hands on her stomach and exclaim with celebration as they witness the wavelike movements of a baby inside. Hannah is surrounded on every side by children. Laughter escapes the chubby- cheeked young ones as they run to her and plead, "Aunt Hannah. Come play, come play…" Penninah looks up from the group of women and, with contempt in her voice, calls the children away. Mockingly, she might have said "Leave Aunt Hannah alone. You know she does not have children! She would not even know what to do with you."

Erupting with her condemning laughter, she turns back to her friends as Hannah slinks away from the scene, completely isolated and embarrassed. The ladies join in Penninah's laughter; the men judge Hannah's husband for staying with her, for she is of no use. They cannot see what God sees. Their eyes only witness a woman in the process, a lady in the "and" space of time, a beauty wasting away with a promise unfulfilled. They see suffering, and though it looked as though it would end her, it was only leading her to surrender.

Like Hannah, there are times when we, too, are in the "between," and we receive criticism instead of comfort because we look undone, haphazard, unpolished. Maybe we cannot keep up with our peers, and their fears of being associated with a failure cause them to move away from us. They talk about all the things we might be doing wrong, the issues that may contribute to our state, when in truth our situation may or may not be due to anything we have or have not done. We may just be in the waiting room of life and our number has yet to be called. We may not have as many social media followers, books written, degrees earned, or the appropriate dog, but we do have a God who is still on our side. While others gape at our mess, the good God we serve does not see promises undone - He sees promises underway.

> God does not need us to keep up with others. He needs us to know that He is keeping up with us,

and His timing is always perfect.

Baby Blues

I can certainly identify with Hannah. I also wanted to have a baby. My husband and I had our daughter, Heaven, in our fifth year of marriage, and as we reached our tenth year, I wanted another child. I figured, "Hey, why not? How hard could it be?" I saw myself as a young spring chicken and felt this would be effortless, especially after having one child already.

The first year I enjoyed all the efforts of conception. I was not concerned at all when I did not become pregnant. I figured I just needed to slow down. We had just planted our church, and I thought stress kept me from getting pregnant. However, as year two crawled its way to a close, my reality went through a metamorphosis. Instead of just enjoying the intimacy of marriage, I thought only about getting pregnant. I tried to time my ovulation just right. I tried to gain control of the situation by eating oatmeal, taking supplements, wearing out my doctor, hounding the internet, seeing the acupuncturist and the natural doctor, listening to old wives' tales and superstitions, and constantly pressuring my husband – as if he were the person responsible for this delay.

I was anxious but not quite ready to throw in the towel. My doctor said not to worry, she would run some tests. I was great with that response and still had a belly of hope waiting to be filled with a life of possibility. The tests showed I had a low progesterone reading of 0.4 instead of the needed 12. I was a little jaded but not dissuaded, and I begin to take a pill designed to increase my progesterone. This in turn was supposed to increase the release of my eggs.

After the first round of pills, I was excited. I simply could not wait for the results of my next test. It was with full confidence that I walked into my doctor's office filled with faith from the prayers I had offered up to God that morning. Nothing can steal my faith, I thought to myself. That is, until she read the results. The medication had caused a decline in my progesterone levels instead of an increase. The doctor was baffled. After all, this pill worked on the majority of women. Why, oh why, did I have to be the minority?

That moment broke me. I felt like a loser, and the claws of disappointment climbed up the walls of my fragile heart. Tears filled my eyes as I asked to stop the medication. It made no sense. I felt like I was in elementary school again being the last one picked for the team. Instead, I was a pastor of a thriving church and I really just wanted to tell my doctor she did not know what she was doing. In reality, though, I saw the truth. My doctor was nice and sweet and educated, so instead of scolding her, I searched for the right "Christian" response, though in that moment being a Christian was the furthest thing from my mind. The powerful prayers of the morning faded away as my pity party ensemble summoned through my hopelessness. Yes, that quickly I stopped believing. Yes, one report pushed my head into the sand. Outwardly, I carried on while inwardly, I struggled to have faith, going back and forth between knowing God could make this happen and completely giving up on His promise for me.

The third year began – still no baby. I had my blood drawn frequently in hopes of tracking down the problem. Low progesterone readings continued. Worry plagued my mind because I saw no change in the situation. One unwelcomed bad report after another found its way to me. Week after week, this went on. Even though deep down, I knew I would have another child, I stopped listening to hope. All the evidence was contrary to that hope, and I became comfortable in the state of believing but not receiving. Like a ballroom waltz, the synchronizing of my emotions with the negative reports began cradling one another in a sad, dark dance.

Winter

The table was cold and rigid. I could not remember the last time I felt such a chill crawl up my spine. Another day, another test. This one was much more uncomfortable and invasive than the others. I felt vulnerable and exposed. They inserted dye into my uterus in hopes that the technician could locate "spillage." I had no idea what that meant, but gathered it would indicate whether or not my tubes were functional.

The results came in and the words "inconclusive," "failed," "non-responsive," "acute," "abnormal," and "INFERTILE" cut me to the core. The report read like a bad newspaper. My tubes were probably collapsed, damaged, blocked, and incapable, as the doctors were unable to get a proper reading from the test. After the second attempt with the same result, the technician refused to perform another test for fear of doing irreparable damage. Like my tubes, my faith collapsed. I felt like a crumpled piece of paper in the hand of a giant. I folded and I wanted to scream at the top of my lungs at this treachery. I felt betrayed by my body, immature in my faith, and weak in my resolve. It was as if I were treading in deep snow, unable to find my footing. My faith and I were freezing over.

I was angry, and instead of understanding the process of waiting on God and allowing the wait to accomplish anything, I became bitter. This preacher was bitter. I became sour within the wait, disappointed by the delay, infuriated by impatience, and fueled by frustration. I was so jealous of everyone else who was getting pregnant. I did not wish them any evil; I just wanted to be them. I longed to celebrate and chat about cravings. Gaining those extra pounds and lamenting about the changes of pregnancy were things I actually looked forward to. I envied the growing bellies of the women around me. My "Christian pastoral" self was happy for them, but the unfiltered me, the me in the dark, the me when I was alone, the private me (that wrestled) was downright miserable. I was envious. My abundant heart that began the process with a fullness now became impoverished.

> **You see envy comes from a place of lack. It believes there isn't enough for you so you want after what someone else has. It tricks you into believing God's account is little.**

I was trying to hold on to an abundant dream from a severely impoverished heart. I'm telling you friends, sincerely, I got weary in the waiting.

God is Gracious

I knew in my head and through experience that God is gracious. I knew He would perform His Word and pardon our sins. But I could not find my footing in my faith, and instead fell into self-loathing. I had not always made good choices. I had endured abuses, taken wrong turns, been caught in and caught up in situations that hurt me, and sometimes, I hurt others. Even though I was a Christian, I was not exempt from some of the damaging decisions that immaturity and neediness had motivated me to make. Like anyone, I had to pay a price, deal with consequences, and walk things out. But here in this situation, after waiting all these years, I could not help but feel abandoned by God, judged by others, and unworthy within myself. I knew better than to feel this way, but I chose not to help it. I felt worse than ever and began getting used to feeling bad than good. I honestly just could not get a grip on my emotions. My emotions ran over me like a stampede, and I got trampled underfoot. I was tired of waiting on God. Like Hannah, I was morphing into an ogre of a person who still went to church, but who was poisoned in her heart. I acted righteous outwardly, but I was not right on the inside. I became mean, short-tempered, and lost. I desperately needed help.

So I sought counseling, accountability, and good friendships. I found myself back in an amazing place of closeness to the Lord. My heart had the opportunity in the hand of God to be restored and to feel hope again. I served the Lord more, loved Him deeper, and I came to truly understand how He is a friend to the brokenhearted. I was never perfect, but at my core, I wanted to please the God I served, for He had saved me. I sought His presence more than prosperity, His face more than my failures, and His approval more than the applause of others.

Yet, even there in that place of sweet restoration, the enemy still assaulted me with judgment and regret over every mistake and wrong choice I had ever made. The lies he fed me attempted to wedge their way between God and me. In my mind I heard, God is punishing you, Sara; your barrenness is proof. God is teaching you a lesson, you little rebellious twit. I listened intently to these lies. Maybe it is true, I thought. Maybe I do not deserve this baby. I am unworthy and warring in this purgatory. I reflected on the women of the Bible and absorbed their pain from being childless, but paid no attention to the end result of their stories – which was grace.

Instead of mercy, I felt God made me pay all over again for what the blood of Jesus had covered. This is what deranged discouragement looks like. It makes you believe crazy things like God is making you pay. That simply is not true. Yet, I bought the lie that I was cursed with barrenness and that I would never be good enough for God to give me the desires of my heart. My heart became sick.

Proverbs 13:12 says, Hope deferred makes the heart sick; but when dreams come true at last, there is life and joy. (TLB) This was the sickness in my heart. I backslid again into hopelessness and started to believe in a punitive God instead of the God that I had known all this time – a God who is patient and loving. A God who is a rewarder of those that diligently seek him.

Has that ever happened to you? Have you doubted God even after all the good you saw Him do in your life? You have seen Him come through for you before. You have seen Him rescue you yet with all that history and evidence you allowed doubt to come in and steal your faith. Trust me, I know how that feels. I tried to use my acts of service as a bargaining chip with God, yet my self-righteousness got me nowhere. I tried to manipulate Him, figuring that if I mustered enough pity, God would have to hear me. I shook my hands at the sky and said, "It seems unfair that those who do not want babies get them, and here I am serving, giving, doing my part in the kingdom, and I cannot get pregnant. Why do you hide your goodness from me? God, where are you? It does not pay to do the right thing." I retreated… again.

And I cried.

I cried that cry; you know the one. I looked in the mirror and tried to summon my most pitiful face. I furrowed my brow and kept my eyes open until the dryness made them red and evoked tears. I felt sorry for myself and said all the right things to feed hopelessness so the cry could have more impact: "I must be evil. God does not really love me. What have I done to Him? Nothing good ever happens to me. I have always been the one to lose."

Drama

Have you ever done something like that, planned the exact moment you would heave and melt down with quivering lips, have a headache and running mascara to make it all look legitimate? Yes, for me, this was the cry that would rival Chicken Little's "The sky is falling!" Personally, I mastered "the cry" and probably could give a tutorial because I am such a drama queen! This agonizing waiting season made me cry. In fact, I chose to cry through pretty much most of this season. I cried so much that I actually categorized the various teary episodes. Let me share:

The Barely: The cry that is just enough to say, "I am still holding on!"...usually done in a worship setting when I plead my case before God.

The Envy: A cry that carries complaining as its best friend.

The Furious George: A very angry cry that is short and terse, coupled with an "I am done" attitude.

The Melt: This is the mega cry. You must have a mirror, tissue strewn about, lamenting practiced, and absolutely no spectators.

Funny thing about this crying business - it does not change a thing! Why? Because

> faith is not activated by a cry, it is activated by a choice to believe.

We all have to wait. There is no going around this established principle. Just look at the Law of Growth, for example. We have to wait to grow from three feet to five feet, right? We have to wait in traffic, in the grocery line, for healing in broken places, in school, at work, and in this God-life that we live. Everything requires an element of waiting, a period of suspension.

To everything there is a season, and a time to every purpose under the heaven. Ecclesiastes 3:1, KJV

Yet God has made everything beautiful for its own time. He has planted eternity in the human heart, but even so, people cannot see the whole scope of God's work from beginning to end. Ecclesiastes 3:11, NLT

The Bible makes it clear that waiting is not some game God chooses to play; waiting is actually a vital process and season through which all great and beautiful things must go through.

> If you and I are in the waiting period of a promise, we are also in the middle of being made beautiful.

Sometimes it is hard to see how this ugly point in time can become glorious, but it is in this place of waiting that we learn to surrender to God the precious things that our heart would otherwise hold onto.

Waiting makes us…

Naked – this is when we become more aware of our true need for God. We are stripped of pretenses and become fully honest with ourselves. After kicking and screaming, pouting and fussing, the person we pretended to be now has to take a step back so that the person God is making us into will be available. Emptying ourselves is a by-product of waiting.

Decided – The opportunity to decide on our operating in our flesh or our faith becomes a real choice. Waiting brings us to the valley of decision. Moving forward, staying stuck or retreating are options from which we can choose.

Humbled – If we are open to the Sovereign imprint of God during our season of waiting, we will recognize He is El Elyon, the Most High God and He has the final say. We accept it is a privilege to walk this life with His Spirit within us and once the reality sets in that we are not alone, it brings an awe in our hearts.

Strong – Waiting breeds fortitude. It fosters a resolve to move forward, regardless of our feelings and sets us on the path of maturity.

The wonderful thing is, if you know where you are in the waiting, you will see how much closer you are to winning. Every step you and I take forward is one step closer to our promise, and every step backward takes us closer to our past. So we must keep moving forward.

My husband shared a scripture with me when my past cashed in on my present, and my disappointment curtailed my determination: "And we know that all things work together for good to them that love God, to them who are the called according to his purpose." Romans 8:28, KJV

After he shared this scripture with me, my husband said with great care, "Sweet, if all things work together for your good, it is only a matter of time before God makes it good for you and glorious for Him. Hang in there." (I just love him.)

That is my encouragement to you, too. Hang in there, friend! It is not over yet. You can win while waiting and win because you waited. Hannah poured her heart out. She endured the waiting, passed the tests of persecution, poured her heart to the Lord, believed in Him and in her earnest plea she made a vow to God. She promised to give back her firstborn Samuel to serve in the temple of the Lord. God answered Hannah's prayer and she became pregnant within the first year giving birth to Samuel who would become one of the most influential prophets in the Bible. The wonderful thing is God did not stop with Samuel. Hannah had five more children! God exceeded Hannah's expectations. Hannah waited and won and so can you.

The Facts of Life

As I went through this waiting period. The evidence the doctors gave me spoke more volumes to me than my faith. Have you had a startling or unforeseen circumstance to come your way? Maybe it's a spouse walking away from the marriage, which seems so surreal. It's hard to even believe this is actually happening to you. You turn to God for an answer. Should you stand and believe for marital restoration or do you yield to the forces of marital separation? You decide to stand in faith. You are praying yet you are not seeing any results. I am here to tell you, "Don't give up." This may just be your waiting period.

Perhaps you have a daughter or son who just cannot seem to get past the bad influences at school or a teacher who is making their life difficult. They are telling you, your child is out of control, he's not retaining the information, she is a troublemaker or the school has just given up on them. Now, you are waiting for a change while resisting the facts. Let me encourage you for a second. Here are some of my medical records. Some of the facts in writing were from doctors who could only tell me the evidence they saw. They reported what was physically before them. But you and I know, faith changes facts. I want to share this with you so you can locate the facts in your life and then understand that regardless of what is opposing you it serves as an opportunity for God to get involved if you will have the courage to walk through the process and wait for the change. Remember, faith changes facts. Oh Baby Oh!

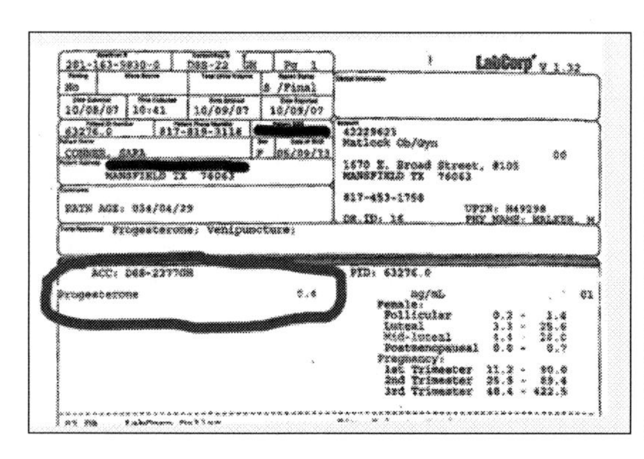

LabCorp

S /Final

10/08/07 | 10:41 | 10/09/07 | 10/09/07

Matlock Ob/Gyn

1670 E. Broad Street, #105
MANSFIELD TX 76063

MANSFIELD TX 76063

Progesterone; Venipuncture;

Progesterone

ng/mL
Female:
Follicular
Luteal
Mid-luteal
Postmenopausal
Pregnancy:
1st Trimester
2nd Trimester
3rd Trimester

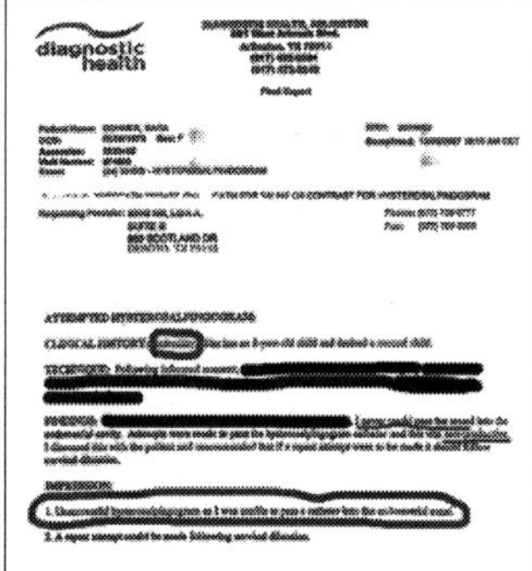

diagnostic health

Oh Baby Oh!

On August 25, 2009, I gave birth to a baby boy named Landon, weighing 8lbs. 12oz! No medication. No surgeries. No complications. Absolutely INCREDIBLE! Landon is a miracle from God that leaves my heart full every day as I reflect on His goodness. As you can see from Landon's picture, his radiant smile lights up the room.

Yes, I waited for Landon but I've also had to wait on many other things in my life besides Landon. I waited on my family to know Christ. I waited on my mother to overcome her 15-plus years of addiction to crack cocaine. I waited on God to provide financial rescues when my husband lost his job due to a back injury. I waited on God to set the right timing for us to pastor a church. I waited on old relationships to be restored and new ones to be made. Yes, I waited on some things, things I knew that God had declared with His Word over my life, things I knew God had spoken through the mouths of others, or things I knew God had whispered directly to my heart. These things took time. Some of them are still taking time, but I had to learn what Paul speaks of in Hebrews 10:35-36:

> "Cast not away therefore your confidence, which hath great recompense of reward. For ye have need of patience, that, after ye have done the will of God, ye might receive the promise." (KJV)

Do not throw away your confidence in the waiting. That's what the enemy of our soul wants you and I to do. But we are in control of our confidence. We can stay strong when we remember, Romans 2:11 says "…there is no respect of persons with God." (KJV) What He has done in my life, He is able and willing to do in yours as well. You may not be waiting on a baby. It may be a business. A husband. A wife. A successful surgery. A court case to be overturned in your favor. Child support. A restored relationship with a friend. A miracle in your credit. A job. No matter what it is, the same process and principles apply. The facts say, "not enough" but

> God is telling you right now on this page, just hold steady. He is working it out.

Exercise patience in God; His promises will come to pass.

Practical Application

While there are principles that contribute to your ability to thrive while you wait, there are also a few questions you can answer to help bring definition to where you are right now within that process. Let us talk for a bit.

Tell me, where are you in your journey between here and there?

Consider It

List some of the facts that you are facing.

I may not be using none of my degrees.

I haven't yet exercised my walk in purpose

Frienships have been seperated

Me and my dad still have growing to do.

How would your life change if those facts were reversed?

If I knew w/o a doubt my purpose
I could make more sound decisions but
I know I need to not let feeling
not good enough stop my progression.

Do you have an 'ugly' cry? Describe it and then tell me if the situation changed after you heaved and hollered. I am just asking.

Yes, I feel like I released
some heaviness. But it also
makes me realize why are you
doing all this when God is
with you haha

Do you feel undeserving of God's promise? If so, what is it you are holding over your head?

Sometimes I am scared of not
knowing if people will respect me
because I don't know what I'm talking
about. I think its because I was
always underestimated in school.

God has decided to partner with your faith. Now that you have laid your cards on the table so you can see them for yourself, have you decided enough with the crying and hurt feelings? Is it time for change?

If you agree with this statement write today's date down below: "By an act of my will, I have decided today to not give up or give in. I will believe God until my change comes."

Today's Date: 11/20/17 Signature: Barbara

Internalize It

Meditate on and memorize this scripture by tomorrow:

Therefore, there is now no condemnation for those who are in Christ Jesus. Romans 8:1, NIV

Speak It

"Because I am in Christ, there is no condemnation for me. All my sins are forgiven and the blood of Jesus cleanses my conscience from every dead work. I am whole, free, and fully loved by God. I am not ashamed. I can boldly believe God to turn my situation around."

Apply It

Do you recognize that the enemy wants to separate us from the heart of God? God's desires for you are revealed in this scripture:

"I have come that they may have life, and have it to the full." John 10:10b, NIV

After reading this verse, you can understand God's intent is for you to live life to the fullest. Do one thing that will bring joy to you (go to a play, take a trip, write a poem, ride a bike etc.). What will you do?

Play tennis w/ my mom
Go to the pool with my brother
Write a poem
Cook a new meal for others
Talk w/ my sisters, Go on a trip!
Hug my friends

Three

Safe Space

True story: It was my older brother's birthday and we were excited to have cake. Seriously. We grew up in a Rastafarian home and one of our main beliefs and requirements was not drinking or eating processed or unnatural foods. That said, we did not eat dessert regularly as dessert was considered a special treat an "occasion food." I don't recall us ever baking anything but chicken. Due to this belief, our passion for birthday cake was immense. My brother Che (yes, that is his entire name) got the knife, and with a swift cut, hit the handle on our green glass table. A chip and a crack later, the table was still functional, but its strength and integrity were compromised. We saw the crack caused by the incident, but since the table could contain the weight of the cake and several other dishes, we carried on as usual for months.

Until that day, that is, the glorious day my vanity got the best of me. I wanted to see myself in a mirror. I mean, if you are going to be cute, you might as well look at yourself, right? The only problem was that the mirror was on a wall across from the glass table. I was not tall enough to see myself in the mirror, and since seeing myself was such a dire need, I had to do something. I had an amazing idea. It was one of those moments where even I was impressed by my brilliance! The glass table. I should definitely get on top of the glass table. It was far enough away from the mirror that I could see most of myself in it if I stood up on top of the table…wouldn't that be grand? Without a second thought, I leapt upon that green glass table and began to pose. Darling. Yes. Vogue it out, honey. Hands on hips, chin up, back arched, how about a walk on the table? That would be even better, do it – and so I did. I strutted down my glass runway, left shimmy, right shimmy, stop and pose. I stood photo ready right on top of the crack my brother created a few months ago. The table began to break, and then break it did, with me right on top of it. I jumped off quickly and do not recall any personal injury, but I do remember the shattered glass and my dad's fury toward my poor older brother who was not even there during my personal glass fashion show, yet was somehow responsible for this catastrophe.

What really happened here? Outside of the obvious "no sensible child should be walking on a dining table--utter failure--" the truth was clear. The integrity of the table had been compromised by a previous incident; it could not handle the pressure, demand, nor weight I put on it. It collapsed not because it was a poorly constructed table, but because it had been weakened and could no longer function at maximum capacity.

Some of us think God is like that table. He is not. He is a safe space. Due to our lapses in judgment, compromises in integrity, and bad behavior, we think He cannot withstand the demand our current desires put on His promises. We feel in some way that our actions impact His ability to perform His Word. We think our failures diminish His faithfulness and our mistakes exempt us from miracles. It is this kind of deception that keeps us from trusting implicitly in the promises of God. Our shames serve as a veil separating us from His love because we constantly focus on our past stupidities.

Though it may be hard to admit, sometimes it is easier to believe that God will fail, that He will not come through for us, or that He will falter. It is easier to believe that God will fall short instead of standing firmly on His promises. Why? Because we fear being let down. Subconsciously, we give God human characteristics and filter Him through our own disappointing experiences. Accustomed to broken promises from others and unfulfilled commitments within ourselves, the supernatural God we serve, becomes in our minds, more natural than super. This belief creates a conflict in our faith. We tally our shortcomings and justify the false notion that we do not deserve His kindness. Since we would not bless ourselves knowing all we know about ourselves, we are not convinced that God would bless us either. However, God is not like us. Though He understands the human heart, He is not limited to, contained in, or defined by the human heart. In fact,

> He delights to work in our lives in spite of our heart. That is GRACE.

Amazing Grace

God is not a man, that he should lie; neither the son of man, that he should repent: hath he said, and shall he not do it? or hath he spoken, and shall he not make it good? Numbers 23:19, KJV

The truth is, God is not a glass table. He is not broken, compromised, imperfect, unstable, or fragile. He is not sketchy or shady. His integrity is flawless and His track record faultless. He cannot be broken and is not dysfunctional, wretched, or ratchet. He is incapable of being weakened by our mistakes. He is not intimidated by our insecurities nor jaded by our foolishness. God has no fault line, no sinkhole, no crevice through which His integrity can crumble.

God can handle our imperfections and has made provisions for our imperfections through the death and resurrection of Jesus Christ.

As a matter of a fact, our strengths were never the qualifiers for the blessings of God, just as our weaknesses were never the disqualifiers. If our righteousness or perfection guaranteed God's blessings, we would get prideful. If our failures revoked them, we would be cloaked in condemnation. Neither of these extremes unlocks the one thing needed to bring God's promises to pass: faith in Him, in who He is, and in His ability. Pride precedes a fall and self-exalts, while condemnation robs us of our boldness to approach God.

We qualify for God's blessings based on His goodness, not ours, His faithfulness, not ours. It is because of who He is and not who we are.

He is trustworthy, and our past, present, or future imperfections cannot break His integrity. He simply will do what He says He will do, because He is who He declares Himself to be. We are saved or rescued by grace not because of our own works. The consideration and aid from God comes to us first because of His love for us. This is what we know as saving grace. It simply is there because God is the Lover of our souls not our sin but our souls. As such, He is able, through the sacrifice of Jesus, to forgive us of all our sins, cleanse us through and through of all unrighteousness and restore us. This means He is rooting for us.

The Integrity of God

Even when we are too weak to have any faith left, he remains faithful to us and will help us, for he cannot disown us who are part of himself, and he will always carry out his promises to us. 2 Timothy 2:13, TLB

Faithful is he that calleth you, who also will do it. 1 Thessalonians 5:24, KJV

Our belief in the integrity of God is what allows us to be consistent in our faith in Him. Integrity. The dictionary defines it as, "adherence to moral and ethical principles; soundness of moral character; honesty". [1]Being convinced in our hearts and minds of the complete integrity of God is the **first step** in thriving during the space between.

I face your Temple as I worship, giving thanks to you for all your loving-kindness and your faithfulness, for **your promises are backed by all the honor of your name.** Psalm 138:2, KJV

Isn't that just an incredible scripture? It's like this. When I was growing up, my parents were in the reggae music industry. My father was actually the road manager for the biggest Jamaican reggae superstar in history, the inimitable Bob Marley. Together, my parents ran a company called Talent Corporation. Due to the immense demand of the music business and the kind of fame it carries, I only saw my father in spurts. My mother had gotten addicted to drugs, and their volatile relationship ended in divorce.

The instability of my mother and the absenteeism of my father due to work began to solidify a false belief in my mind: promises are meant to be broken. Based on the situation, I learned that promises can change, they are unreliable and not to be counted on. I came to understand that a promise could only be trusted based on the person making it. If my dad said he was coming home on Tuesday, I would get my hopes up, but a flight delay could make it Wednesday, resulting in disappointment for me.

---

1 http://www.dictionary.com/browse/integrity?s=t

Even though flight delays were out of his control, to a six-year-old who had not seen her father in three months, one more day was an eternity. Sometimes he would tell me I could go with him somewhere and then change his mind. He missed my high school graduation, leaving the day before to go on tour. Growing up like this, I knew that, yes, my father loved me, but his promises were unreliable because, at the time, he was unreliable. To be fair, this was as a result of the entertainment industry he worked in. I am trying to show you how easily an idea can form in your mind and that idea becomes a truth you build your beliefs on. This can all be founded on misconceptions but as a child isn't a lot of what we understand in our simple minds exactly that? Misconceptions.

My birthday is in May, always around Mother's Day, which is a very busy time for musical artists. I am not quite sure, even as I write this, if my father who loves me tremendously, has been around for more than one of my birthdays – and that one was my fortieth. I did not like my father missing my birthdays growing up, but now I understood the demands on his life at the time. My understanding now didn't help my misunderstandings then.

My mother, however, made birthdays a big event - but always with conditions attached. With invitations already sent she would warn, "I will cancel your party if you do not …." And with all my might I tried to be good, but my mischievous mind would get me into trouble, and sure enough, one more birthday would be canceled. I had a few great ones with her and some I looked forward to that got shut down the day before. Those usually came with a lot of yelling and hard spankings.

Consequently, when I got into a relationship with God and was told He is my heavenly parent, I figured He was the same as my earthly parents. I figured He would make promises to shut me up but not really mean what He said. I also assumed that punishment was a guarantee and purgatory was my bonus. I wanted to believe in God and I did. I believed in Him, but I did not really believe Him. I believed in Him for my salvation but did not believe He had reliable motives beyond that. I believed He made the stars, but I did not believe He would do anything beautiful for me.

> I understood His handiwork, but was ignorant about how His heart worked.

Yes, He wanted me to be obedient to get to Heaven, but all the supposed "living a blessed life on earth" stuff was a carrot He dangled in front of me so I would follow Him, a carrot He never intended to let go.

> It is hard to receive from someone you do not believe believes in you.

would tally up my misdeeds, bad thoughts, and annoying attitudes, and always come up short. I compared the weight of my sins against the table of His goodness, and in my mind, my imperfections always trumped His ability to see beyond them, or so I thought. After all, if my Mom, who was supposed to care for me, would cancel my birthday party because I took soda out of the refrigerator, dropped it on my foot, and had to get stitches, how was God supposed to look past my immaturity, forgive my rebellion, or pardon my ignorance? It was hard for me to see the fault line was never in Him, it was in my belief about Him.

Is He Who He Says He Is?

I had to take an uncomfortable leap and make a choice. My parents were flawed. They did the best they knew how with the exposure and resources they had. Their own youth, histories, and experiences played a role in mine. We were not a Christian family. We had no wonderful family Bible studies or church conversations. I was not a pastor's kid, a deacon's daughter, an elder's niece, or a missionary's kinfolk. I did not grow up hearing words like "baptism," "hallelujah," "wash me clean," "praise Him," "all night prayer," or "He brought me through." I didn't know how to shout in the Holy Ghost or have family meetings. I was a heathen living a hedonistic, consistently sinful lifestyle with no moral compass nor conviction. There was no faith example, no restorative 12-step program I could follow, and no holy music playing in our house. I knew to respect my elders but listen, I just didn't.

What am I telling you? We have concepts of life we learned from the people most influential in our lives or the circumstances that impacted us the most. I was the first in my family to commit my life to Christ when I was fourteen years old. At the time, my idea of Father was; fun, funny, exciting, generous, protective but busy. Now, I had to choose. Would I actually believe God the person and not just the title He held? I had to decide to believe God's promises were true and they could be trusted because He was true and could be trusted. This was a learning process. I had to study the Bible. Discover the character of God. Absorb fully in my heart the words of love He left inscribed in the Bible. When I made the decision to believe His promises, my whole world opened up. I received grace, mercy, healing, deliverance, restoration, prosperity – all of it – because I knew that I knew in my noggin that God Himself was faithful, and

even at my worst, He still remains His best.

You have the opportunity right now to take Him at His Word and slam the gavel on doubt. Shake off the disappointment caused by the people in your past who let you down, and stop reducing God to their failures. I'll tell you this. As I got to know God better, He worked on my heart. I prayed and prayed for my family to know Him. Some came a few months later and then years later my Mom gave her heart to Jesus. Two years later at her funeral my bonus mom gave her heart to Him and about a year after that my dad did the same thing. All in all, some of my confusion and false beliefs pushed me to lean in to God more passionately. This led me to eventually get past the lies and wholeheartedly trust God. As young as I was, I trusted Him with my family and after waiting for a while, He answered my prayers.

Give Him a chance by making this choice. The choice of accepting His integrity. Whatever He says He will do, He will do. Today is the day, now is the moment to trust who He is. He is the God who loves, leads, and lavishes us with the best.

> John 3:16 says it so well, "For God so loved the world that He gave His only begotten Son, that whoever believes in Him should not perish but have everlasting life." (NKJV)

He gave up His best so we could have the best. Will you choose to believe that He is who He says He is? He is a faithful Father who never fails. I sincerely hope you will choose who He really is over who you have imagined Him to be based on bias and filters. He indeed is good. He is always good.

Let us pray together:

Father, I come to you with all my disappointments, broken promises, personal failures, and wounds in hand. I confess I have doubted you at times. I understand I do not have to have it all together even if I pretend that I do. You are just waiting for me to surrender my misunderstandings. I am making a choice right now, and I choose YOU. I choose Your love over the lies, Your faithfulness over my fears, Your heart over my hurts. I choose to believe according to your words in John 15:16 that You have chosen me. I know Your integrity is not influenced by my inconsistencies, and love is the only motive in Your heart toward me. Teach me Your ways, reveal to me who You are. I am here, I am listening. I am waiting and I am willing.

Your child ________________,

Practical Application

For many of you, this chapter hit a tender spot in your hearts. Like me, you grew up in an atmosphere where people and their promises could not always be trusted. I spoke about my dad yet my mom was missing for even larger chunks of my life due to her battle with drug addiction. Consistency, reliability or stability were just not part of the deal. But I did have tons of excitement and fun along the way woven in the tough stuff. Inconsistency was more comfortable than consistency and brushing off disappointment was something you just learned to do. Truly trusting God can really be a hurdle if you have been hurt in this way, but we all have to come to this place of trust with Him if we are to fully walk into the promises He has for our lives. How? You have to make a decision. Decide. Resolve. Establish a new code by which you will live and love your live. Conclude as the ultimate truth that God has no error in Him, He is to be trusted and you will believe Him above anyone and anything else. It's really simple, you make a decision every day to do something, so I know you can decide on doing this.

Consider It

Who broke your trust? How is his/her behavior reflected in how you see God?

____

____

____

____

____

Read the above prayer again and then take a moment and write what the Holy Spirit whispers to your heart:

____

____

____

____

____

____

____

____

Are you someone who lacks integrity? I was and in some ways still working on increasing that. For example, not being on time is an integrity issue especially when we say we will be there. Or, making a promise to your child and then because you're tired, you tell them to wait another day. Even in giving your word to yourself that you will workout and then keep pushing it off. This speaks to integrity; honesty and soundness of character. As you meditate on the character of God, allow Him to change you from the inside out. Where can you improve your integrity?

____

____

____

____

____

____

____

Internalize It

Meditate on and memorize this scripture:

"God is not a man, that He should lie, Nor a son of man, that He should repent. Has He said, and will He not do? Or has He spoken, and will He not make it good?" Numbers 23:19, NKJV

Speak It

"Father God, I choose to believe in your integrity. I know that in You, every promise is 'yes and amen'. The things You said are the things You will do. You are completely trustworthy. I lay my fear down at your feet. I pick up hope and I choose to move forward boldly and confidently, believing every word you spoke over my life is true."

Apply It

The Lord is head over heels in Love with you. Do you believe that? Look at this scripture:

"For the Lord your God is living among you. He is a mighty savior. He will take delight in you with gladness. With his love, he will calm all your fears. He will rejoice over you with joyful songs." Zephaniah 3:17, NLT

Write down three things you know in your head to be true, based on this scripture. Then go over those things again and again until you fully believe them in your heart.

1. ____

2. ____

3. ____

You know something that gets on my last nerve? Seriously. When my kids ask me to do something or they ask me to take them somewhere,

Four

Wrong Expections

You know something that gets on my last nerve? Seriously. When my kids ask me to do something or they ask me to take them somewhere, and then have the audacity to have a bad attitude while waiting. It may go a little something like this:

"Mom, I need to go to the craft store. When can we go?"

"Maybe later on today."

Time passes. I may be working on something, cooking, pulling my hair out, or talking to myself, but I am doing something. I am fully aware that we need to go at some point; however, I am not inclined to rush because I was just informed of this need. Without fail, only a short span of time passes before I feel the presence of a child moving in on me...

"Do you know when we can go?"

Thinking about it, I realize it has been all of a glorious five minutes since my child asked me the first time, and I wonder to myself which of her ears I should bite for interrupting me...again.

"Look, you just asked me. I have other things to do; you will have to wait."

"Okay, but do you know how long, though?"

"No. But I am sure it is not in five more minutes. Sometime before the store closes. How about that?"

Then I go back to whatever I was doing. As sure as the moon is in the sky, here this child comes again, sulking, impatient, and a little irritated. The hairs on the back of my neck begin to stand up, and I pray for her sake that she does not approach me again about going to this store. Seriously. No. She has to take the leap of death and venture into the danger zone. Yet here my child comes, brave and foolish, a little ticked, a little salty, and with a whole lot of impatience.

"Mom, I really need to go. I have homework and it is due and I need time to do it and I have to get there and do you know where daddy is? Is there someone else who can take me? How much longer are you going to be; I waited 15 minutes already and I am hungry and I am tired and can we stop to get something to eat after? And I was up early and I need to do my assignment, so can we go?"

What in the world? First of all, I do not work for my children unbeknown to them. Secondly, my child impedes my schedule with her lack of planning, and thirdly, I am not obligated to go anywhere. I feel I have fed her and kept her alive thus far, so surely this request is not on my list of "I have to's" as a parent. Did I mention – I do not work for my children? It is not the impatience that crawls under my skin like a bad case of eczema; it is the huffing and puffing. It is the everlasting complaining and never-ending attitude that make the trip to the store delayed and difficult. By this time, I am in shock, and I have determined that this attitude is going to create an adverse reaction from me. Instead of speeding up, well now I will take my sweet little time because obviously my child needs all the time she can get to return to her right mind. In the end, we did not need to get to this place of conflict. A good thirty minutes of waiting with a great attitude would inspire me to move just a little faster. Not much, but a little.

God doesn't respond to us as I did in that situation as a parent. He is patient. He does not react based on emotions. He is not governed by emotions but by principle. Looking over my life, however, I truly believe my own attitude impacted when and how some of God's promises came to pass.

> **You see, the promise of God can be declared, but its fulfillment is not always automatic.**

Sometimes there is a process tied up in between now and then, and our attitude about this process is key to getting through the process successfully.

Our attitude reveals our disposition, how we respond both emotionally and physically. For example, if I believe a person has something against me, but I honestly do not care, I may express that through indifference. On the other hand, I may care deeply, and show it by being on guard or combative. Let me get more personal....

Growing up, my parents were great individually but not together. There were some wonderful times of being together riding down country roads and raving at concerts into the wee hours of the night. There were Sunday afternoons eating freshly-caught oysters and fried fish and running naked on the beach (that would be me – hey, I was about 5). Sand between my toes and smelling like coconut tanning oil are treasured memories for me. I loved those times. More common, though, were tantrums and flare-ups, meltdowns and aggression, tension and chaos. I did not like those times. Eventually, my parents divorced, and my disposition changed from optimism toward relationships to resignation of the fact that relationships do not all last forever.

After committing my life to Christ as a teen, I got engaged and married at 21. I knew then, just as I know now, that I married the right person. God gave me a promise that He would give me a husband that would love me like Christ loved the Church. I held onto that promise, but my attitude, which was formed years earlier, nagged me on the inside.

Will this last? Is he for real? Why isn't he saying 'I love you' 100 times a day? Is he thinking of me? What is he thinking? Is he going to leave? What did he mean when he said that? Exhausting, right? Absolutely. But because of past experiences, I had doubts. Those doubts created an insatiable desire inside of me for affirmation, approval, and acceptance. The promise, my husband, was right there, but at times I had difficulty receiving the consistency of his love. Though we were spiritually and mentally compatible, emotionally I had gaps I expected him to fill. I grappled with feelings of inadequacy and fell into webs of deception. And yet, he loved me and taught me through it all. There was not an issue with him; there was an insecure attitude within me that kept me stuck, needy, and immature instead of fully yielded and receptive. Over time, though, I got hip to my foolishness, and I began to have a marriage based more on faith than fear. My attitude impacted how I functioned. How I functioned impacted how I responded to the promises of God.

> How I respond to the promise impacts how and when I receive it.

Is it really possible that our answered prayers are affected by our attitudes? I had to dig a little in the Bible to find the answer to this question, because I certainly wanted to know. And it turns out the Bible is filled with people who encountered delays, detours, devastation, and denials – all because they wilted in their attitude while waiting. Our attitude is so important. Look at this example in the Bible because 2 Kings 5 is so crazy interesting! On the one hand a prideful attitude almost cost one person their miracle and on the other hand a feeling of entitlement and impatience cost the other person their destiny. It is so intriguing. Let us dig in.

The Word of God never lacks adventure. The chapter begins by highlighting a problem. Naaman is a lion of a man. He is a great officer in the army and he sits head and shoulders above everyone else. Strong in power but weak in person, he has the debilitating disease of leprosy. Leprosy can lead to amputation, disfigurement, loss of feeling, curling of joints, tumors, and deformity. Naaman commands legions of soldiers and yet he has no control over the lesions in his bones. Neither Naaman's rank, education, contacts, nor fame can rid him of this public and private horror. He desperately needs a miracle from God, a God he does not know but a God who knows him. He needs a breakthrough as his body is breaking down. A servant girl in his house tells Naaman's wife that there is a prophet named Elisha who has the ability from God to heal. Naaman wastes no time. He gets all the paperwork done so he can be on his way to see Elisha. Do you see it? Right there is the beginning of faith. Naaman believes the word of the servant girl and begins reimagining his future. He believes he can get healed and immediately makes preparations to make that healing a reality. He adds action to his faith. But then, when he gets to Elisha's house, Elisha refuses to come outside and greet him!

Let us do a quick review. A maid gets word to Naaman that he can be healed by this prophet. That is the promise. Then the between begins. Naaman makes the effort and goes to see Elisha. He takes gifts, sends a letter to the king, and brings servants. His attitude up to this point includes courage, belief, and faith in something he has heard of but has not seen yet. This reminds me of the scripture

> Hebrews 11:1: "Faith is the substance of things hoped for, the evidence of things not seen." (KJV)

But then, Naaman gets to Elisha's door and Elisha decides he is not coming out to greet Naaman. Instead, Elisha gives Naaman some instructions through a servant: "So Naaman came with his horses and with his chariot, and stood at the door of the house of Elisha. And Elisha sent a messenger unto him, saying, Go and wash in Jordan seven times, and thy flesh shall come again to thee, and thou shalt be clean." 2 Kings 5:9-10, KJV

Let us stop right there. Say what? Naaman left his lofty palace, stopped by the king, dragged his servants along, loaded up camels and donkeys with gifts, and goes all the way to see Elisha, but the prophet does not have the courtesy to come outside? Finger snaps. Head shakes. "No he did not," gasp. Naaman gets so angry that his attitude of faith turns into a festering frustration: "But Naaman was wroth, and went away, and said, Behold, I thought, He will surely come out to me, and stand, and call on the name of the LORD his God, and strike his hand over the place, and recover the leper." (v. 11)

That quickly, Naaman lost sight of the promise, and his faith was interrupted by his bad attitude. His healing was now delayed. Nothing had changed about the promise. In fact, Elisha gave Naaman the secret to being healed. All he needed to do was wash in the Jordan seven times. It was not that complicated! Take a bath seven times in a specific place – that is it! But Naaman did not like the instruction nor the obedience required to receive his healing. He envisioned his healing going an entirely different way, and this was not part of his idea of a healing plan. His pride created a stumbling block in his path.

"Behold, I thought." As it is with Naaman, so it is with us. Usually our opinion is the origin of our funky little attitudes. Our thoughts betray what our hearts pray. The heart believes the promise and the mind just sees the problem. Elisha did not ask Naaman to think anything, Elisha asked Naaman to do something. But Naaman was accustomed to solving problems logically. He was accustomed to things going according to plan. When his assumptions were not met, Naaman's response was to overthink instead of just act. He chose to rely on his head knowledge instead of his heart.

We do this, too! You know the saying "assumption is the mother of all mistakes"?

> When we assume in our thoughts how God should do something, we bring His holiness to our lowliness.

If assumptions are our default response, they will lead to delays when we could just obey. Too often we hear God's promise for our lives and then plan ourselves right out of God's promise with our complaining attitudes and thoughts that lead to disobedience. Somehow we end up blaming God for our promise going unfulfilled, when actually it is our fault for being disobedient.

Naaman focused so much on the Jordan part of the process he became temporarily blind to the promise. That messy, humbling, ugly, junky, inconvenient part had his attention instead of the sentence in verse 10 which clearly promised "and thy flesh shall come again to thee, and thou shalt be clean." The promise had not changed, Naaman's attitude did. As long as Naaman remained prideful, God's promise for him could not come to pass. God wanted to heal Naaman. He gave him a clear directive on how to be healed. It was so simple; all Naaman had to do was his part. His stubborn ideology and feelings of entitlement prolonged the process. The healing was still located at the end of the seventh dip in the Jordan. It hadn't moved. Naaman was not moving towards it until the waiting wore his little will down just enough to listen.

Course Correction

Eventually, one of Naaman's servants had had enough of his moping. This servant came to him with bold humility and asked, *"My father, if the prophet had bid thee do some great thing, wouldest thou not have done it? how much rather then, when he saith to thee, Wash, and be clean?"* 2 Kings 5:13 (KJV)

In that moment, Naaman saw how petty he was. He recognized his pride and corrected his course by arresting his attitude. Making this alteration led to his obedience, and that obedience led to his healing.

This story sure makes it look like a bad attitude while waiting can delay the timing of a promise being fulfilled. Too often we walk away because God nudges us to be obedient in small things and we only want the glory of significant things. But we need to understand that God has a way, a method, and steps for us to follow. They will not always be what we think they should be, but we must decide to trust Him because His plan is always the right plan. My friend, we need to settle in our hearts that

> little instructions can carry great leverage in the Kingdom of God.

The amazing grace of God gives us the opportunity to course correct. There are times when my husband and I are traveling to a destination and our GPS gives us clear directions about how to get to our destination. On the way, we may see something familiar, like a gas station we remember or a store we have been to before. Then we think, Hmm, our destination must be close, and we follow our thoughts instead of the GPS. Usually, we get lost, turned around, or stuck asking for a way back to where we began. When we make that course correction, it may cost us 15 minutes, a little angst, and some gas. The destination did not change, but the time it took to get there certainly did, and all because we did not follow the directions.

Similarly, we often trust God in the beginning, and then somewhere along the way start relying on our own strength. But

> God wants us to invite Him to be our guide for the entire journey, not just part of it.

Thank goodness He always gives us opportunities to course-correct. Often these opportunities come as warnings. Like that velvety automated voice that says "make a legal U-turn", these warnings are the flashes on the screen that tell us to take a different route. When we make the correction, it is called repentance – turning away from one thing and toward something else.

Naaman repented. He ultimately humbled himself and went back to the original instruction. He went to the dirty Jordan River. He bathed seven times, as instructed. God knows what He is doing. We must keep in step with Him. Even though there was a delay, Naaman corrected his course and got his healing.

What about you? Ever had a poor attitude about an instruction God gave to you? Do you see a relationship between disobedience and delay? I am just trying to tell you, we should stop blaming God for the lag time we experience when we know we only gave him partial obedience on the way.

Jumping the Gun

Once Naaman received his healing, he was grateful and humbled. He endured the shame of being in the Jordan, recovered from his haughtiness, and sincerely worshipped God from that point on. To show his appreciation, he offered to give Elisha gifts, but Elisha refused. Desiring to honor God, Naaman loaded two donkeys with dirt from the riverbank so he could worship God on soil from the place where he was healed. This was his way of setting up a memorial, a landmark to signify this new relationship with God. His softened heart was beautiful to behold. His healing was complete and his relationship with God was on fire. Praising and rejoicing, he set off for home. And then…

Here comes drama. Elisha had a servant named Gehazi who had been with him for quite some time. Gehazi had seen miracles performed by Elisha, and as his protégé, he had an inside view of the awesome ways God blessed His people. You see, Gehazi also had a promise, a purpose, and a plan for his life, and he was on track to see it lived out. Yet he too was in a waiting process. While Naaman's journey looked like sacrifice and submission, Gehazi's looked like service and stewardship. He was a servant to Elisha and a steward of that anointing and authority.

Elisha also had served his mentor, the prophet Elijah as a faithful son. As a reward for his faithfulness, Elisha asked for a double portion of Elijah's spirit (2 Kings 2:1-15). Sometimes people interpret this as a double measure, as in "twice as much." This term "double portion," however, is better understood as a term of inheritance, meaning Elisha wanted to be as the firstborn among the sons of Elijah. When given to one of his sons, the cloak, or "mantle," that the prophet wore established that son as the one with the double portion, just as with a natural firstborn son and his father. All the blessings, authority, manifestations, responsibilities, and duties that went with Elijah's prophetic position were given to Elisha.

This kind of legacy was a pattern in the Bible. Moses, the great Israelite deliverer who led Israel for 40 years, had a son named Gershon, but it was Joshua, his servant "son," who received the double portion, making him the leader of Israel. Joseph was Jacob's eleventh son, but he was the favored and chosen one. The cloak he received established him as the firstborn, entitling him to the double portion and his father's authority. This was a natural and spiritual custom (Deut. 21:17).

Gehazi understood this principle of the double portion. He knew the favor that would come with such recognition and influence. He is the one mentioned the most with Elisha. He was the ride or die, ace boom, day one kind of servant son. Based on the established patterns, Gehazi would assumedly be the next major prophet. He was the obvious choice for the mantle. But the process was not moving quickly enough for him – he wanted to help it along. I mean, if you already know what is meant to be yours, why not just grab it now instead of waiting until later? Everything was set for Gehazi…until his desires outpaced his patience:

> "But Gehazi, Elisha's servant, said to himself, "My master shouldn't have let this fellow get away without taking his gifts. I will chase after him and get something from him." 2 Kings 5:20, TLB

Destroying Your Destiny

The perspective with which Gehazi viewed what was happening around him created an untimely desire within him. This desire, when struck, ran hot with the need to be appreciated, noticed, validated, and individualized. It is like someone who serves in the church nursery without being noticed, or someone assisting in a department who knows full well she has the most experience and is confused about why her promotion would be passed over, or someone who is the bridesmaid one too many times. They grow tired of seeing the blessings around them but not in their hands. They know the blessing is theirs, but they do not get why no one else sees that – so they push to just make it happen. Maybe then they will be seen and finally get what they deserve. Ever had this attitude? I am telling you now, it is vital for us to understand that

> the scarcity or surplus of what is happening within us is more important than what is happening to us.

Because we think what God has for us is more important than what He is doing within us. BUT what He is doing within us is the very thing that will help us steward the manifestation of the promise He made to us. Proof of this lies in the end of Gehazi's story...

He ran quickly and caught up to Naaman, who was on his way back home. Gehazi was running with such urgent strides that Naaman leapt off his chariot, worried something was wrong. Breathing heavily and waving his arms, Gehazi finally calmed down and charmingly assured Naaman that all was well. He told him that he and Elisha had some guests, so Elisha had sent him to get some money and two robes to host these (imaginary) people. Well, how could Naaman refuse after being healed? He already had a desire to give and burst with joy at the opportunity to express his gratitude. With a heart of generosity, Naaman gave Gehazi more than he asked. This is the double-portioned life I am talking about, Gehazi mused to himself as he sauntered back to his quarters. The hot breeze licked his face as he imagined himself wrapped in silk robes, the royal colors finally making him a standout.

When Gehazi arrived home, he hid the gifts and acted as if nothing happened...like a spouse who goes over budget while shopping, stuffing bags in the trunk of the car, the attic closet, behind the bushes, or at a friend's house...as if online banking does not exist. Anyhow –

spoiler alert! – this does not end well. Elisha, who had stayed behind, asked Gehazi where he had been. I keep thinking with my 21st-century mind that Elisha had the "find my phone" app tracking Gehazi, but no, this was a real prophet who heard God, saw things, knew things – out-of-this-world stuff.

Gehazi acts puzzled and confused, wrinkling his brow and shaking his head. No, absolutely not, I did not go anywhere. Elisha, you are imagining things. It is okay though, you are getting up there in age. Nope, did not go anywhere at all. If this was a movie, the dramatic and tense musical score would slowly rise. The piano would capture the base tones and the stringed instruments would carve out an eerie sound. The picture would dim and a perfectly choreographed lightning storm would appear after a loud crack of thunder. In pure horror fashion, you would grip the hand of the person next to you as the gloomy, creepy, please-do not-do-it, brace back, squeeze eyes, shake-your-head terror grabs your bones and you groan at the screen, "No, Gehazi, no!" Your shoulders would slump as he delivers his line in an English accent, "Thy servant went no whither." 2 Kings 5:25b, KJV

That always puzzles me, by the way…movies about the Bible with British-accented actors who are portraying Middle Eastern characters. Hilarious. Anyway, back to the drama…

It is a stab to the heart as we see Gehazi's promise retreating. We ache as we watch his future being robbed by the rush of impatience. Popcorn drops from our hands as we watch how calmly Elisha stands. His hem sweeps the floor and the dust rises ever so slightly as one sandaled foot takes a weighty step forward. It is as though your bones shake with the authority felt within that one step. You can barely breathe. You know Gehazi's heart races while his deceptive mind tries to calm him. He does not have the courage to look at Elisha, and Elisha does not need any courage to do what he has to do. A pause. A moment being offered for Gehazi to tell the truth, to change his attitude, to surrender. Will he take it? Come on, Gehazi, course correct. But no. With one final step, Elisha's deep, careful, and strong voice states,

"Went not mine heart with thee, when the man turned again from his chariot to meet thee? Is it a time to receive money, and to receive garments, and oliveyards, and vineyards, and sheep, and oxen, and menservants, and maidservants? The leprosy therefore of Naaman shall cleave unto thee, and unto thy seed for ever." And he went out from his presence a leper as white as snow." 2 Kings 5:26-27, KJV

Our jaws drop and our hearts sink. Everything disintegrates like burning paper, and we can not do anything about it. Though we try to catch it, those pieces crumble within our fingers. How close they were, Gehazi and Elisha. So close that Elisha could say his heart went with Gehazi. It could not have been easy for Elisha to execute that judgment, and in my mind's eye I glimpse Gehazi realizing the gifts he took prematurely were not worth the years of shame, exile and disregard he was about to experience as a leper. The respect he once had as a servant son was now replaced with ridicule as an outcast.

The Bible does not state a successor for Elisha. It simply mentions that King Joash was by his side when he lay dying. Gehazi could have received the double portion, but his impatient and greedy attitude cost him and his family dearly. God had a promise. God had a purpose. God had a plan. That plan was good. But Gehazi got impatient in the between. Being a go-getter in the wrong season gets you more than what you bargain for. Sometimes a hold up in our timeline is really a holding out for our obedience. Gehazi left the presence of Elisha in a leprous, unrepentant state. While Naaman's impatience and ignorance delayed his promise, Gehazi's immaturity and refusal to accept responsibility denied him his promise completely. It is so important to monitor our attitudes, for attitudes can impact us greatly. We must remember that

> an attitude of obedience puts us in the queue for promotion.

Practical Application

Time for an attitude check. Do you try to take things into your own hands because you are impatient?______Yes ______ No ______ Sometimes

Consider It

Think about a time when you had a bad attitude which may have slowed down a promise being fulfilled in your life. What happened? Spill the beans.

____

____

____

____

____

How can you correct yourself so this does not happen again in the future?

____

____

____

____

____

What are some other attitudes (besides the ones outlined in this chapter) that you think may affect the timing of the fulfilment of God's destiny for your life?

____

____

____

____

Internalize It

Meditate on and memorize this scripture:

You must all be quick to listen, slow to speak, and slow to get angry. James 1:19, NLT

Speak It

"I declare I am the obedient. My trust is in the perfect God and His perfect plan for me. I am not afraid of waiting. I am up for the journey for I do not walk alone. I will fulfill His will for me. I will live my best life. I will see the promises of God come to pass. I am committed to a submitted heart when I don't understand the way. My attitude is one of joy and gratitude."

Apply It

Walking an obedient life begins with willingness.

If you have a willing attitude and obey, then you will again eat the good crops of the land.Isaiah 1:19ESV

Do you have some "I'll nevers" that can hinder your obedience? For example, "I'll never forgive them.", "God ask me anything but that!", "I'll never move to Alaska." Like Naaman, what is your Jordan and are you willing to forego your preference for His perfect will?

Five

Backspaces

Delay can be misinterpreted as slothfulness on God's part. When we view delay this way, we may attempt to fix the "problem" ourselves, not knowing that the root of this action is fear…fear that God will let us down. Some of the things that trip us up in the middle are unresolved or neglected issues that can create bigger problems. When the pressure seems too great we forget about the previous victories God has manifested in our lives. When waiting begins to extract out of us what we don't think we have to give, if we are not careful we can make the situation worse. You and I may be in a hard place and if we're not mindful and intentionally focused on God's promises instead of encouraging and building ourselves up, we end up reverting backwards; digging ourselves into a deeper hole.

DIY

Have you ever seen a Do It Yourself photo on a website and figure your project will look exactly the same? Take for example cabinets. There is a choice to install them professionally or with your hammer and web photo in hand you decide to go for it yourself. Only later do you realize DIY projects don't always come out the way you imagined because the person who actually posted the photo was an expert! This is one of the ways we mishandle the space between.

Genesis 16 tells of the matriarch Sarah, Abraham's wife, who had a promise from God. God sent angels from heaven and told Sarah she would have a child. Well that was just plain crazy! Sarah was already old and well past her childbearing years, and yet, God said she would be the mother of all nations. As she got older, she could not intellectually figure out how God would bring this promise to pass. Her body bore the signs of barrenness.

Physically, her decline spoke to her more vividly than the promise heaven had declared to her. Her hope waned and her logic got the best of her. "I am old. I am withering. The time has passed for me to bear children. I am forgotten but I will not forget – I am owed a child." Sarah decided to fix the situation on her own. She gave her servant Hagar to Abraham as a second wife so he could have a son. I believe Sarah's motives were out of love for her husband and wanting an heir to carry on his name.

> But good intentions do not make wrong actions right.

Sometimes you can have a perfect heart and still use imperfect methods. The path of impatience can take us away from the place of obedience.

Restlessness gave way to recklessness. Ishmael was born to Abraham and Hagar, but he was not the promise, he was a reminder of the problems:

- Sarah still had not given birth on her own.
- She was too old to bear sons.
- She still waited for the true promise to be fulfilled.

Ishmael was a beautiful boy born into a bad situation. Eventually, God did fulfill His promise, and Sarah had her own child, but Ishmael was a lifelong reminder of her impatience. Truly, do you think if Sarah knew that on such-and-such date she would give birth to her own son that she would have given Hagar to her husband? Probably not. We do not always know the exact time God will move, but we have to determine to believe that He will do the things He promised. It is

better to wait than to bear the weight of poor decisions.

Forgetfulness

The disciples in Matthew 14 had an in-between experience as well. Jesus made a promise to meet them on the other side of the lake. During their journey from the one shore to the other, a storm arose. Had the storm come on before they cast off, they could have decided to never leave the safety of the lake's shore. If the storm raged at the completion of the journey the disciples could have run for cover. But of course, the storm blew in like a tempest right smack in the middle of the lake, too far to turn around and too close to the end to quit.

Sometimes that happens to us. We are on our way to the other side of our problem and on the brink of attaining what we know God promised. We trust God and then, BOOM, a storm hits us. Maybe our marriage gets rocky, our job is cut, our supervisor is stressful, our emotions are spent, our cellulite escapes the girdle…*storms*. The funny thing about storms is they often come right after the calm.

As someone who grew up in the Caribbean, I have experience with what we call "hurricane season." Hurricane season is a regular cycle experienced by people who live in the region of the West Indies. We endure tropical storms and raging winds from hurricanes. In the center of the hurricane is the eye. When the eye passes over, all seems well. It can be calm, sunny, and undisturbed. Then, moments later, harsh winds can whip through the city unapologetically.

The disciples had just left an incredible place of miracles where they saw Jesus feed thousands of people with a few loaves and two fish. They witnessed Him taking little and making it much. Not only were they witnesses, they participated. They were there as the majestic power of God accomplished the impossible. It was as though they were in a calm, a triumphant place of success and increase. A few moments later, the storm came. Quickly, the disciples reacted in fear and forgot the miraculous things done moments before. Terror overtook the testimony they just experienced. Jesus was on the lake watching them, but the disciples were blinded by the severity of the storm. Their attitude of faith turned into forgetfulness and fear. Once in fear, they strained, and just wanted to survive.

Ever been there, in a place where a storm came suddenly and you had blessing amnesia and forgot the goodness of God, a place where you were thrown into full-blown panic? I have. The waves got boisterous. Jesus walked on the water toward the boat. Upon seeing Peter, He called on him to take a chance and trust Him in the middle of the storm. He asked Peter to get out the boat and walk toward Him. As Peter walked on the water toward Jesus, he became distracted by another gust of wind and began to sink. But then he got things back on track when he cried out to Jesus to save him. Then, after Jesus was invited into the boat, the winds and waves ceased.

When a storm comes into our life, our first reaction may be to look at the possible destruction, to think over and over about the negative outcomes. Panic and stress can throw us into straining attempts to rescue ourselves by leaning on what we know instead of the God we know. Storms are a part of the journey, but how we handle them is in our control. We must remember the promise of Hebrews 13:5, that God will never leave us nor forsake us. It is up to us to see that Jesus is already on the shore watching, because He is fully convinced we will make it through the storm.

It may be scary and chaotic, but I truly believe that when we keep in the forefront of our mind the victories God has performed in our lives, it helps us remember we are not victims in any situation.

> **If we made it through with Him before, we will make it through again.**

Whatever God has called you to, He is certainly bent on getting you through whatever He needs to in order to get you to the other side.

The fact is, Jesus was on the lake watching the disciples even when they were unaware. You have to know God would not give us instructions if He did not know we were able to complete them. He will not give us a vision that He is not ready to bring to pass. He sees the end from the beginning. So if an unexpected storm comes in the middle of your journey, understand that God is in charge of the wind and the waves. He has full confidence in you to complete the trip. Keep remembering the battles you already won, and it will help you in the current battle you are trying to win. Forgetting God while waiting on Him only creates more distance between you and your "other side."

In the space below, write down a promise, vision, or instruction God has given to you. Then write down any opposition, difficulty, or difficult people you encountered that opposed, discouraged, or persecuted you along the way. In the third space, write what you learned or observed along the way. Finally, what decision did you make after passing through the storm? Who did God show Himself to be during the journey? You will notice you learned something new about yourself and something new about God when you take the time to remember.

Worry

When the hard stuff comes, we usually do not want to deal with it. We resist valleys and deserts, storms and dry seasons. We resent being a little ahead of where we were but not quite where we believe we could be. Yet, can I just tell you sincerely? It is possible to thrive between mountains and flourish in hard places. We do not have to be afraid of what the journey may bring because we are engineered by God to excel in every season. We were born to win. God installed the very best into our DNA, and we are coded to overcome the adversity life throws our way. We are given beautiful examples in the Bible and in nature announcing this truth: We have the capacity to grow when the odds are against us.

Difficulty is a revealer. It pulls away the curtain of what we think we are capable of and gives us the opportunity to reveal abilities we never would tap into if we did not have the need. The cactus plant gives us a vivid example of this. While it waits for its next refreshing of water, it learns to weather arid conditions. There is a reservoir built within it that stores water. Cacti do not question if they can endure. They do not run from the sun or bury themselves in the sand. There is a confidence in a cactus that rises out of each stalwart, spiny needle, standing in brave defiance of the desert. Cacti do not question their ability to survive. They welcome the dry seasons and are not intimidated while waiting for the next rainfall, for they are certain it will come. They simply need to wait out the season they are in. You and I share that same comfort…trouble does not last forever, so let us not invite it to overstay its season with our negativity and faithless attitudes. Instead, let us hold out stalwart faith, and believe that "this too shall pass."

Complaining

Our impatience with God's process shows up in several ways, but **complaining** is the most common. Proverbs 18:7 says, "A fool's mouth is his destruction, and his lips are the snare of his soul." (KJV) Murmuring, griping, and whining expose the lies we have bought into based on our insecurities; the lies that God will not fulfill His promises, that He has forgotten us, that maybe He really cannot come through for us.

When we become deceived like this, we end up criticizing God, the very One who can help us most. This deception is dangerous.

> **God is not moved by our complaints; He is moved by our faith.**

Our kicking up a fuss and throwing hissy fits reap results we cannot calculate at the time. God does not appreciate grumbling. He takes grumbling as a personal affront to His integrity, as it is a sure sign of unbelief. Look at the following story about the Israelites to weigh this claim for yourself…

In Exodus 3:8, God lays out His promise to take the Israelites to a "land flowing with milk and honey." To a people who were enslaved and deprived of the best Egypt had to offer, this was an incredible hope. Even though the Hittites were in the Promised Land when the Israelites arrived at its borders, the fact that God had promised this land to them should be a clear sign that they would be victorious and take it as their own.

Upon arrival, Moses sent out 12 spies to assess the people and land of Canaan. After forty days, the spies came back with a report. Ten of them said,

"We be not able to go up against the people; for they are stronger than we. And they brought up an evil report…we were in our own sight as grasshoppers, and so we were in their sight." Numbers 13:31-33, KJV

This report was evil not because it was not factual, but because it revealed the spies' lack of trust in God with the statement, "we were in our own sight." By saying that, their faith in God's sight came into question. It showed that they valued their own assessment over the assurance of God. In that moment, they settled for the "facts," they retreated from courage, and they forgot and disdained all that God had done for them up until that point.

Though two of the spies, Joshua and Caleb, stood up for God's promise, the Israelites decided to believe the testimony of the other ten. Their hearts melted like wax, and the mission came in second to their misguided emotions. As their thoughts caused a fearful retreat, their mouths declared words of ingratitude and insult. "Why would God bring us out here to die? Egypt was better; we should have stayed and died there," they lamented. Their complaining triggered God's displeasure.

Hebrews 11:6 notes, "Without faith it is impossible to please him: for he that cometh to God must believe that he is, and that he is a rewarder of them that diligently seek him." (KJV)

God was not pleased with the people. The words they uttered totally misrepresented His heart. He brought them out of Egypt because of His compassion. He delivered them from Pharaoh because of His love. He provided for them the spoils of their oppressors because of His goodness. But the negative confessions of their mouths ensnared them. God said to Moses, *"How long will these people treat me with contempt? Will they never believe me, even after all the miraculous signs I have done among them?"* Numbers 14:11, NLT

The Israelites filled their mouths with complaints instead of clinging to the promises of God. Yes, they would have to get rid of the people in Canaan. It absolutely would cost something, no matter what. The takeover would not happen overnight. The "milk and honey" life would take time to come to pass. They should have realized that, with God, they were clearly on the winning team! They opted out and chose to stand still through complaint rather than move forward with conviction in God's delivering truth. God wanted even more for them than they desired for themselves. But their lips made a covenant with their situation. They swallowed the diet of Egypt, that life of barely getting by, of struggle, of never-enough, of weightiness. Their imaginations would not reach beyond their experience, and so neither did they. In the end,

> their words of doubt, complaint, and unbelief sabotaged their future

and God said to them: *"As surely as I live, declares the Lord,* ***I will do to you the very things I heard you say.*** *You will all drop dead in this wilderness! Because* **you complained against me,** *every one of you who is twenty years old or older and was included in the registration will die. You will not enter and occupy the land I swore to give you. The only exceptions will be Caleb son of Jephunneh and Joshua son of Nun. You said your children would be carried off as plunder. Well, I will bring them safely into the land, and they will enjoy what you have despised. But as for you, you will drop dead in this wilderness.* Numbers 14:28-32, NLT

Hold on did you catch that? God told them He would do what they said! They made a covenant with their lips and set in course their future. God did not take back His promise, but it was postponed for an entire generation. They verbalized an alternate outcome and it manifested. We have got to watch what we are saying when we are waiting. God's heart never changed, the people's heart changed. We get upset about the results of our actions and have the audacity to blame those results on God or the devil.

Faithless complainers were uninvited to the Promised Land. The result of their complaining was very painful. Numbers 14 goes on to tell us that 40 years of wandering resulted as a consequence for their unbelief, one year for each day the spies had spent exploring the Promised Land. It was through those forty years of drawing circles in the sand that the younger generation learned to wait on God and believe in His promises; as the complaining generation died out. This young generation, ruled by Joshua, went on to achieve mighty things in God because they were fueled by faith instead of unbelief. They learned that it was best not to complain while waiting, for they had seen firsthand among their fathers and mothers that complaining delayed the best things from coming forth.

Are you a complainer? Let us take a little test. Here is what complaining sounds like:

- Why is this happening to me?
- I do not see God providing.
- I am sick of this.
- This is never going to change.
- I wish I could go back to…

Are you guilty of having any of these thoughts or speaking any of these words?

Take a moment to search your heart. If you say any of these things (or have other complaints), repent and fill your mouth with faith filled words instead. *Declare you will succeed. You will come through better than you went in.* ***You will win!***

Impatience

Another big roadblock to seeing God's promises come to pass is **impatience.** Moses is a great example of impatience. Dealing with the complaining Israelites in the desert and fighting with thirst had Moses just a tad frustrated. He approached God about finding water, and God told him to speak to the rock. As the people continued to whine, Moses added a little grumbling speech of his own about their ingratitude. Moses called the people "rebels", and instead of speaking to the rock, he lifted his rod to the sky, and with all his pent-up frustration, he struck the rock twice. Water gushed out to satisfy the people's thirst.

There, they got water. Moses helped them get it. It looked like a win. But no, God was not a happy camper. He had His own way of getting the water – speak to the rock – but Moses' impatience with the people motivated him to make his point. He had had it up to his neck with all the complaining. I can imagine him saying, "You ungrateful degenerates. With God, I got you out of slavery, brought you through the sea, and took you this far, but all I hear is your nagging mouths. I am sick of it. If it were I, I would leave all y'all trifling, childish people." He was exhausted from the complaining. As a result, Moses led the Israelites out of the place of persecution, but never into the land of promise.

I have moments as a leader in my home, my church, and my community where I find myself impatient with others. I always judge my own intentions well, but not so much the intentions of others. Unwittingly narcissistic, I look amazing to myself because I know I mean well; however, I am not as quick to extend that gracious perspective to others. In the end, that impatience and intolerance has injured and insulted people, occasionally causing my influence to swing more toward the side of ineffective instead of inspirational.

Ultimately, impatience is birthed out of the idea of insufficiency. When you believe there is not enough, you will be tempted to fill the distance between where you are and where you need to be with self-designed methods. You rush to fill the gap with manipulation, judgment, or fix-it-myself impatience. But here is the thing: God has not called us to fill in the gap; He has called us to stand in the gap for others. He will fill the gap. This is where so many of us falter, just like Moses did.

> We forget that how it gets done is just as important as getting it done.

When the in-between seems to drag on, insert trust. We must understand that there is always specific timing with God.

Are you impatient? Let us take another little test. Here is what impatience sounds like:

- I will fix it myself.
- If I hurry, I will get ahead.
- I am tired of waiting.
- It is taking too long.

Are you guilty of having thoughts like these? While we are in repentance mode, let us take these to God, too. We must replace our thoughts with His. We find His thoughts in the Word of God.

Comparison

Comparison is another way to get sidetracked in our in-between seasons. It's easy to look at the harvest seasons in the lives of others and forget that they had to endure a winter season to get there. Having not been invited to the b-roll of their edited lives, we sink into our chairs and bitterly watch the highlight reel. Comparison is like a fungus that grows on your confidence, causing it to become stale. It begs for attention and craves shortcuts. The root of comparison is insecurity, so it feeds our need to be significant by having us focus on the applause of men rather than the approval of God. In the end, comparison will cause us to compromise who we are for the sake of keeping up with others.

> The problem with comparison is that someone always loses – usually the person who starts the contest.

Comparison brings out the worst parts of ourselves because we tear somebody down (either ourselves or someone else) so we can continue in our victim roles or enjoy being the victor at someone else's expense. Truly, playing the comparison game is one of the greatest disservices we can do to ourselves.

We compare our weight, our marriages, our wealth, and our children. Yes, we even drag our children into this chaos, pushing them hard to excel not so they can better themselves, but so they can be better than the children of our friends. One of the things I did not realize I did was compare my childhood experience to the childhood of my children. I made this comparison as if constantly doing so would breed gratitude. I would say, "When I was growing up, we did not have electricity sometimes," hoping this would create grateful attitudes in my kids. Instead, it only created puzzled looks. In trying to create gratitude, I fostered confusion. How could they relate to a life they had never lived? I ultimately realized that gratitude was not going to be built in my kids by forcing my past realities upon them. It would be taught by directing praise for our current blessings toward God and living a lifestyle of thankfulness in front of them.

Comparison can push us out of season. We do not want to be left behind; therefore,

> we settle for something less instead of staying the course for something greater.

We settle for a relationship that is not good, because it is better to have a person who loves us a little than to have no one at all. We content ourselves with scraps and sacrifice what is best for what is barely there just so life will not pass us by. We do not want to be judged. We have FOMO (fear of missing out). We want to prove we are not failures. We want to silence our critics, make our punishers pay, live a better life, get ahead. I get it. I do. But the funny thing about God's process is that He does not skip grades. If we compare, it is a sign we are not ready to graduate from our current season, because our focus is on what is happening around us instead of what is being cultivated within us.

> Rivalry does not push us forward; it tears us apart.

The path of comparison does not get us ahead; it actually just leaves us behind the next person to whom we compare ourselves.

"For we dare not make ourselves of the number, or compare ourselves with some that commend themselves: but they measuring themselves by themselves, and comparing themselves among themselves, are not wise." 2 Corinthians 10:12, KJV

God does not think comparison is wise. Run your own race. When you run while looking at others, it is only a matter of time before you get out of your lane, trip over a hurdle, or fall behind. **You cannot run forward looking sideways.** Just cheer instead of compare. Comparison feeds the lie that God does not have enough affection for us. It decreases our self-worth and makes us project onto God the idea that He is unfair and preferential. Comparison will not work when waiting on God. If we believe these lies, then no matter what God is doing in us, for us, and through us, we will never have enough and never feel enough. If we accept this not-enough perspective, we lose confidence, and if we do not have confidence in God, we have no faith. If we have no faith, nothing becomes possible, and we are left to fend for ourselves. We will recite "woe is me" prayers instead of bold ones. We will ask for little and fall prey to the strategy of the devil, which is to separate us from God. How can we believe Him, trust Him, and love Him if we believe we are always on the short end of His love? This in itself is the worst position to be in – to serve a God you do not believe is for you.

Do you struggle with comparison? Here is what it sounds like:

- I wish we had a house like that.
- I wonder why God is blessing them.
- What did she do to get him?
- It is because of who they know.
- He is just lucky.
- Those things never happen for me.

I feel led by the Spirit of God right now to pray for all of you who felt betrayed by God because He blessed someone else, for those of you who feel less-than because you think someone else is getting more. Even though you know God doesn't betray. Cast down these lies right now in the Name of Jesus. Hold this scripture in your heart:

"The Lord hath appeared unto me of old saying, Yea, I have loved thee with an everlasting love: therefore with lovingkindness have I drawn thee." Jeremiah 31:3, KJV

Let us pray:

Father, I set my faith in agreement right now that the readers of this book will receive the love you have for them, this everlasting, unending, full and pure love that puts them at the forefront of your mind and in the center of your heart. I pray they will put down their wheelbarrows of worry and surrender their fears to you. I ask for your peace to wash over them now as they continue waiting in strong expectation for your faithful Word to come to pass in their lives. In Jesus' Name. Amen.

Ungratefulness

In Jamaica, we have loads of fruit trees all over the island – crisp Chinese jimbilin, suede-like naseberries, stubbornly plump star apples, sticky and sweet pineapples, and a plethora of mangoes. There are the tall East Indian mangoes, the sweet Bombays you can twist off and eat with a spoon, the hardy Black mangoes, and the sweet Julie mangoes. When I visit Jamaica, there are two things I want to do right away. The first is eat my favorite meal of oxtail, rice & peas, plantains, shredded vegetables, and macaroni salad at Ziggy's restaurant in Kingston... yes, all at once, all on the plate, all of it until the food is stuffed up to my eyeballs. (Glutton, yes. But that is my first greasy stop, hands down.) Then, I want to eat fruit. More specifically, I want mangoes and my kids want guineps, which are small, round, green fruits the size of large grapes.

At the very first fruit stall we can find, we jump out of the car and begin our pickings. My kids leap with joy at the bunch of guineps ready for purchase. I keep looking...something must be wrong! I just flew from Texas with a desire so strong I jumped countries to satisfy it. I do not see them. Where in tarnation are the mangoes? "Sorry miss, de mango, dem nah bear right now, ah nuh mango season; you haffi wait." You heard that right – "Sorry miss, the mangoes are not bearing right now, it is not the season for it; you will have to wait." I can look at my kids and begrudge the blessing that their fruit is in season, OR I can celebrate with them, partake of it, and wait for my mango season. I have eaten mangoes out of season in America and Jamaica. The same holds true in both countries: a raw, unripe mango will hurt your stomach, and one that is force-ripened lacks sweetness. For the ripe, juicy, sweet mangoes that I love, I had to wait for their proper season.

Israel faced the same thing when they wanted a king. They looked at all the other nations and said to Samuel, *"No!... We want a king over us. Then we will be like all the other nations, with a king to lead us and to go out before us and fight our battles."* 1 Samuel 8:19-20, NIV

They complained, then compared, then in their ungratefulness, they constructed a plan to replace the King of Heaven with a king on earth. Taking matters into their own hands instead of trusting the Master's plan created havoc for them.

Ungratefulness is ugly. We need to

> recognize that the blessings in the lives of those around us serve as an indication of what God is able to do for us, not of what He withholds from us.

Our friend Scott Thomas said, "If God is blessing my neighbor, it means He is in the neighborhood." We too have a due season, and it is coming. We must know in our hearts: a season of waiting always precedes a season of harvest. Let us be grateful in our current season.

Disobedience

There is a divine timing of God also known as an "appointed time." This timing has more to do with a place in God rather than an age in Him. It refers to a maturation process and an ability to discern God's direction at a particular time. This type of maturity regards obeying

God as the most important thing. Prompt obedience brings us closer to Him while disobedience draws us further away. We must guard our hearts to keep them from being strangled by disobedience.

"Until the time came to fulfill his dreams, the LORD tested Joseph's character." Psalm 105:19, NLT

Joseph had a God-dream, a vision-- that certainly came from God-- about being a ruler one day. The dream was clear; it was certain and sure. However, the day he received the dream was not the day he was sent out to fulfill it. Joseph had to be tried, tested, and matured. Many difficult situations came his way: He was blamed for crimes he did not commit; he was imprisoned; he was overlooked; he was ignored; he was betrayed. All of these things came to either break him or build him.

Joseph's dream, while a God-given one, was greater than his immediate ability to carry it out. His heart had to be tried so his character could be developed. When my eight-year-old child says he wants to be a firefighter, I cheer him on, but I do not sign him up at the fire academy! No way! It is obvious – he is too young; the gear is too heavy; he has no experience or wisdom. This is how it is with us and God. He has a precise timing attached to the dreams He births within us. This is not necessarily a chronological time as much as it is a space in time. Meaning, God has an individual path for us all. Marriage may be on that path. You may choose a mate at 20 years old and be mature enough. It could be a God directed marriage; in perfect timing. For another person, their journey may take them to 30 years old. Both of these scenarios for the Christian includes the Sovereign factor of God being involved, the maturity of the believer relative to the purpose on their lives and the level of obedience along the way. The 30 year old may have lived in great obedience and the spouse is revealed at that time but disobedience could have pushed it to 36 years old. In other words it is not a standard that every spouse must be revealed at 30 years old and if you're not married you have missed God. No. Our task is to get in step with Him and allow our character to develop while we are walking.

> What God has scheduled for us; our faith and obedience will take us to it.

Personally, I found that I may not be aware of my immaturity in a specific area until I fail a test…like getting offended at someone's lies about me, or their gossip, or their mistreatment. I want to lash out, return an eye for an eye. At times, I overestimate my own ability to manage my emotions, to think spiritually, and to process with wisdom. Usually, I believe I am well capable, and then someone or something frustrates me and I resort to fleshly tactics and bouts of self-pity. It is then that I understand some promotions in my life have not made their way to me yet because I still value the approval of others more than being obedient and Christ-like in my character. Like Joseph, my character is tried. At times, Christ in me shows up and at other times, my flesh wins. It is then that I realize the truth:

> It is not my physical age that qualifies me for promotion; it is the quality of my obedience to God's word.

Quality because we mistake partial obedience as enough when it still is disobedience. Joseph is not recorded as being offended, bitter, angry, spiteful, complacent, isolated, or afraid. As a prisoner, he gave his best. As a manager, he did his best for his boss. As a Prime Minister, he loved his best. Despite all of the difficult times that he faced, Joseph surrendered His heart, and this is what eventually brought forth his promotions in God. Though He was young based on the lifespan of people at that time, His obedience kept him in a cycle of promotion.

With every level of promotion came persecution. But he remained faithful.

Un-forgiveness

The final roadblock to your promise is unforgiveness. Unforgiveness ends up causing too many of us to fall short of the destiny God has ordained for us. Look at a parable Jesus told as our biblical example of this:

"Therefore, the kingdom of heaven is like a king who wanted to settle accounts with his servants. As he began the settlement, a man who owed him ten thousand bags of gold was brought to him. Since he was not able to pay, the master ordered that he and his wife and his children and all that he had be sold to repay the debt.

"At this the servant fell on his knees before him. 'Be patient with me,' he begged, 'and I will pay back everything.' The servant's master took pity on him, canceled the debt and let him go.

"But when that servant went out, he found one of his fellow servants who owed him a hundred silver coins. He grabbed him and began to choke him. 'Pay back what you owe me!' he demanded.

"His fellow servant fell to his knees and begged him, 'Be patient with me, and I will pay it back.'

"But he refused. Instead, he went off and had the man thrown into prison until he could pay the debt. When the other servants saw what had happened, they were outraged and went and told their master everything that had happened.

"Then the master called the servant in. 'You wicked servant,' he said, 'I canceled all that debt of yours because you begged me to. Shouldn't you have had mercy on your fellow servant just as I had on you?' In anger his master handed him over to the jailers to be tortured, until he should pay back all he owed.

"This is how my heavenly Father will treat each of you unless you forgive your brother or sister from your heart." Matthew 18:23-35, NIV

We must not allow an unforgiving heart to keep us imprisoned and locked away from enjoying the promise of peace, health, prosperity, companionship, promotion, or wholeness.

> Sometimes the shortest distance between you and your dream is a decision to forgive someone.

When we do not forgive people, we put them in the most influential position in our lives. We hold on to them. We let the effects of their offense control us, influence us, and motivate us. We esteem them so highly that we reject God's command to forgive. They become so important that we disobey God – so you see – they become the main influence on our lives. We think that by not forgiving them we are belittling them, punishing them, and holding them hostage. But no, we give them prestige and power. We show the world that they are so valuable and important in our lives that we just cannot let them go. But we must.

How do you let go the person who hurt you?

1. Realize we all fall short.

2. Remember God is a Healer.

3. Reimagine your future with the healthy relationships God has for you. The new people can't come in as long as you're holding on to the old.

4. Release forgiveness because you yourself have needed forgiveness from God.

5. Redeem the time you've lost being mad over this by sinking yourself into your purpose, your hustle, your job, your relationship with God. When you are consumed with God and what He wants

you to do you won't be caught up in unforgiveness. You just won't have the time.

6. Recite the word over your mind "Father, Hebrews 9:14 states the blood of Jesus will purge my conscience from all dead works. This is a dead work. Thank you for the blood of Jesus cleaning my mind, my soul and my heart now in Jesus' Name."

7. Refocus on something else worth focusing on. This doesn't bring you any joy so stop rehearsing it and giving it authority by constantly bringing it up. He or she is gone. They have moved on. They're smiling in their photos. Stop the guessing, ifs, ands, or buts and pull yourself up.

We must forgive others, not because they deserve it, but because we realize we did not deserve forgiveness from God, and yet He was merciful. Forgiveness does not let them off the hook, it just hooks you up to the best God has for you by choosing the best way forward… His way. We forgive to show God that He is preeminent, and we trust Him to handle justice for us. We must believe that God will act on our behalf.

"Jehovah himself is caring for you! He is your defender." Psalm 121:5, TLB

Do not Give Up

Let us not get tired of doing what is good. At the right time we will reap a harvest of blessing if we do not give up. Galatians 6:9, NLT

We cannot give up. We must guard our hearts from the promise thieves and continue doing what is good and what is right even when everything seems wrong.

> God has a harvest in mind even in the middle of your hard time.

Change your view. Perch on high and get perspective from where He is seated. Watch alongside the heavenly hosts cheering you on, for they know that in just a little while – not much longer now if you can jump the hurdles of impatience, complaining, and mistrust – you will win. You will resist bitterness and envy. Your heart will burst with gratitude, and in its full state, your promise will make its way to you, anchored on a foundation of faith and hope, upon which it will thrive.

Practical Application

Praise God that He has given us so many examples in the Bible of how not to attain a promise! These examples sure do give us a great guide about what actions and attitudes to avoid. The fact is your Father in Heaven wants you to succeed. His forgiveness is abundant. His mercies are new every morning. But we still have a responsibility to be careful and to be aware of the roadblocks that stand between us and Him. We must rely on His grace. Allowing Him to fully teach us His ways instead of letting our fears, anxieties, comparisons, or worries rule our lives.

Consider It

Which of the roadblocks in this chapter do you think may hinder you from attaining your promise? Are there others that were not listed in this chapter?

____

____

____

____

____

____

____

Is there a person you need to forgive? If so, who and why?

Is holding onto offense worth wandering around in circles and away from your next promotion in God?

Think about something amazing that God did in your life in the past. Bring it back to remembrance. What was it? Can you thank Him for it again now?

Internalize It

Meditate on and memorize this scripture:

"'If you can'?" said Jesus. "Everything is possible for one who believes." Mark 9:23 NIV

Speak It

"Dear God, I admit that I tried to do things in my own strength. No more. You are the strength that I need. I confess that at times I have forgotten what you have done for me and started to worry because of my unbelief. No more. I will remember the things you have done in my past and I will believe for even greater miracles in the future. I know that I have been impatient and jumped ahead of where You wanted me to be. No more. I will wait on You. Lord, I know I have complained and compared myself to others. No more. You are a good Father, and You give me exactly what I need and You made me perfect in every way."

Apply It

Did you know that the grace of God does more than just redeem our souls? It is also His life-giving power that enables us to become like Him and to do all that He has called us to do. Ask God for His grace to show up. Whether it is the grace to serve. The grace to sow. The grace to separate. The grace to stand or the grace for supernatural miracles. His grace is available in our weakness, in our wandering and in our waiting.

But he said to me, "My grace is sufficient for you, for my power is made perfect in weakness." Therefore I will boast all the more gladly about my weaknesses, so that Christ's power may rest on me. 2 Corinthians 12:9, NIV

Six

Wind Power

I have had the chance to go sailing a couple of times and one of the things you have to be careful with is the sails. If they are not positioned properly the wind will not be used to propel the sailboat forward. The wind uses resistance to push it in the direction it should go. Waiting is a form of resistance.

> **It is pulling something out of you, building something within you all the while with the intention of you going forward.**

Just as we can do things that will prolong our season of waiting, there are ways to get right in step with the Spirit, ways to gain an advantage when it comes to reaching toward your desired promise in God. It is all tied up in the way in which we wait. We get acceleration power to push us forward when we engage in the proper attitudes that engage the power of the Spirit.

We have walked through some stuff by the time you have reached this chapter. We know waiting is part of the process. We understand that the danger of impatient waiting creates delays, detours and in the event of an unrepentant heart, denial. We have searched our hearts to see if we can locate the attitudes that hinder us from making progress. So now let's get to the nitty-gritty.

There is a way we should wait. This helps us stay in step with God. This helps us stay right on target and in season positioning us to receive God's promises in the right time.

We must wait in faith and not frustration. This is the FIRST attitude we must possess. In faith means in God's word, with God's word and on God's word.

"Then you will not become spiritually dull and indifferent. Instead, you will follow the example of those who are going to inherit God's promises ***because of their faith and endurance."*** Hebrews 6:12, NLT

Faith. There are so many views of it. It can seem like some hokus-pokus, dilly-dallying business or some ethereal concept too difficult to grasp. But if we dig into it, the Bible gives us a wonderful explanation of faith that is really quite simple. Foundationally speaking, Hebrews 11:1 says,

"Now faith is the substance of things hoped for, the evidence of things not seen." (KJV)

Let us break this down a bit. "Faith is the substance." The word substance here means "the foundation." It also means "beginning." It is the beginning of things being hoped for or expected. It is the first thing.

Now run with me over to John 1:1: "In the beginning was the Word, and the Word was with God, and the Word was God." (NIV) The same Greek word for "substance" is used for "beginning" in John 1:1. John declares the Word as the beginning, the substance, the first thing. Follow me just a while longer. Head over to Genesis so we can see how this Word which was in the beginning actually played out:

In the beginning God created the heaven and the earth. And the earth was without form, and void; and darkness was upon the face of the deep. And the Spirit of God

moved upon the face of the waters. And God said, Let there be light: and there was light. Genesis 1:1-3, KJV

Faith is the beginning, and the Word was in the beginning. Faith is the foundation. Faith is the Word of God. God saw the earth as void and without form. However, He had an expectation, a hope to see it in a different state. He said what He desired. His Word is so strong that it has the power of creation within it. God's Word pulls all things into subjection and alignment with His creative desires; His Will.

When we are waiting on the promises of God to come to pass, we have to be conscious of two things:

1. The promise is designed within itself with the ability to come to pass.
2. God's Word spoken activates the promise.

Faith, therefore, is the Word of God. That is why "the just shall live by faith" (Heb.10:38, KJV). It is why Hebrews 11:3 says, "Through faith we understand that the worlds were framed by the word of God, so that things which are seen were not made of things which do appear." (KJV)

We will not have an advantage during our seasons of waiting if the Word of God is not believed and spoken.

> Believing in God's Word is believing in God.

When we speak words of faithlessness, those words slow down the process, hinder our belief, and activate doubt, which is the stalling agent of faith. However, when we follow the pattern of God by understanding and believing what He has promised, we speak His words, knowing fully that they are coded with the precise information needed to bring into our present realm what currently only exists in the invisible.

Faith and Patience

Hello Sara,

I thought I would write a short Confession for you to say daily 3 times a day just as you would take medicine.

I Sara am a joyful mother of Children and my Children are like olive plants around my table and Eben and I have the wisdom of God to direct their lives. In Jesus name

Longer version

Father in Jesus name I thank You For your word that declares Children are like arrows in our hands and you promised to make the barren woman a joyful mother of children and that my children shall be as olive plants around my table. I thank You that I will not Cast my fruit before the time because I am a tither. I thank You Father when Eben and I come together you bless my womb and cause children to come forth. I speak to my body and I command Everything that is out of order to get in line with the Word. In Jesus Name I am a mother of many!!! Amen

You may desire to have a baby like I did and are facing impossible odds. Instead of doubting, comparing, and whining, you need to find God's word for your situation and begin to declare His word. Do not become obsessed with it – obsession is a means of control and you are not trying to control the situation because honestly you are unable to do so. Pastor Bridget Hilliard gave me a handwritten confession to speak over my situation. I have included it below but incase it is hard to read here is what it says, "I Sara (put your name) am a joyful mother of children and my children are like olive plants around my table and Eben (put your spouse's name) and I have the wisdom to direct their lives in Jesus' Name." Then rest in the truth that God's

Word works because He is faithful. While you are speaking your word of faith make sure to be doing works of faith in preparation. If it is a business, you can confess but you also have to register that business, have a business plan or at the very least do some research.

Simplifying this, we see that waiting on God's promise with "faith and patience" means believing God's Word fully and not being agitated, no matter how long it takes. Patience. Being in undisturbed peace while enduring, while waiting…this is patience. Patience is not being ruffled by anything because you are sure of the end result of the thing you are believing will happen.

In the Bible, those who inherited the promises understood this:

For the vision is yet for an appointed time, but at the end it shall speak, and not lie: though it tarry, wait for it; because it will surely come, it will not tarry. Habakkuk 2:3, KJV

Worship

The in-betweens are often discouraging. Too many of us do not make it through the in-betweens unscathed. I know I have bouts of anger, stress, anxiety, jealousy, envy, and every evil thing plague my mind when I am in the valley of between. I cry. I slump and honestly question the worth of it all sometimes. If I do not watch it, depression covers me like a wet cloak, and the talons of despair pull me into a darkness that scares me. So you see, writing this book not only strengthens you, but it strengthens me too. I must stay vigilant when I want to escape. I must push forward when I want to curl up, roll over, and play dead. I must find a way through when I am exhausted and irritated. I usually reach this melancholy state after weighing the facts and disregarding God's Word. I get weary when I am negligent in my time with God. It is a fact…when I slack on worship, I suffer while waiting.

> **Worship takes the focus off of me, my situation, and my struggle, and instead puts it on God's strength, His love, and His sovereignty.**

Worship allows me to rein in a foul perspective and cast forth a perspective of faith instead. Worship gets to the core of my lack and leads me into a place of plenty. Taking the time to bow before God moves me away from the altar of my problems.

Taking the time to worship is absolutely key to getting an advantage. It is through worship that:

- God brings supernatural help. (Acts 16:16-40)
- Joy is received (joy brings strength). (Psalm 16:11, Neh. 8:10)
- God is exalted. (Psalm 113:4)
- The outcome of a situation can be changed. (2 Chronicles 20)
- We pour out our hearts. (Psalm 142:2)
- Exhaustion is healed and protection is received. (Psalm 61:2-3)
- God's presence is felt. (Revelation 21:3)
- God gives us rest. (Exodus 33:14)
- God gives direction. (Genesis 28:15)

Worship is the currency of Heaven. It bridges the natural and the supernatural. It is the most sacred of sacraments. The greatest privilege of the human believer is to have an audience with His Majesty. To walk among angels and stroll past divine creatures, to offer our tears, our heartbreaks, our admiration and affection – what an honor. Worship allows us a face-to-face conference with the most powerful Being in the universe. It whisks us into a suspended hold of affection spanning eons of time as we fall into the arms of grace and speak with raw abandon, even if it is in hushed words, to the God we also call our Father.

Waiting without worship breaks you to pieces. It is parched and dry. The way is course and the journey hard. Worship is what brings you into communion with the Holy Spirit. It is what alerts Heaven to cheer you on, angels to run alongside you. At the end of it all, worship says to God, "I need You; I know You; I want You; and I believe You." Then God is moved and strength to endure is passed on from His presence to our hearts. Worship is an activator. Moses worshipped on Mt. Horeb when he saw the burning bush and received direction. Abraham worshipped on Mt. Moriah and received provision. Jacob worshipped at Bethel and received protection. Paul and Silas worshipped in the jail and received deliverance. Jesus worshipped in the wilderness and the hosts of heaven ministered strength unto Him.

> It is foolish to think we can get a God ordained result without including God.

We include Him when we invite Him through worship.

Remember

Nothing brightens a dreary day like sunshine, and nothing lifts the discouraged heart like gratitude. In my marriage, there are times when I think, "Did I read the fine print?" When my husband and I are at odds with each other, or I feel slighted and uncared for, I have to press past my feelings of "ugh, this man though…" to something better. In order to not allow my emotions to take me down a road of bitterness and resentment, I have to grab a weapon of remembering. I begin to list all the good things about my husband, like how he considers me in practical ways like filling my tank with gas, or surprising me with a trip, or putting up his plate. As I meditate on the great things, I find that my anger subsides and my gratitude rises. Before long, I do not see him as an enemy but as a promise God gave me. This, dear friends, has helped me from saying stupid stuff and damaging the relationship. It has brought me to the apology table and allowed me to value being reconciled over being right.

> Gratitude builds up God's résumé in your mind.

When you make a list of what He has done so far in your life, of what or who He has saved you from, of how He has turned bad circumstances into stones of strength – this builds your courage and fortifies your confidence in Him.

David did this very thing when facing the biggest challenge of His life. Just imagine David, a bit impetuous, ruddy from being in the sun day after day, and with the confidence of a person who spent time with God. His life in the pastures allowed him to spend long hours strumming tunes of comfort on his harp. He walked with the sheep while speaking with the Shepherd of his soul. Over time, David grew to truly know His God. He had built a relationship with Him. Alone with God, he had overcome some threatening circumstances and lived to tell about them. The promise of God on His life was to be King. On his journey he encounters being a shepherd, then he is faced with Goliath and the warrior in him is being developed. All of this is happening during the space between. On the way, He encounters proving moments. Moments that challenge his faith in God and moments that God uses to reveal Himself to David. It is these previous victories that give him the boldness to stand up against Goliath. In this opportunity, He recites the victories, He recalls his experiences and He remembers God's deliverance in the face of those who doubt him.

"Your servant has killed both the lion and the bear; this uncircumcised Philistine will be like one of them, because he has defied the armies of the living God. The Lord who rescued me from the paw of the lion and the paw of the bear will rescue me from the hand of this Philistine." Saul said to David, "Go, and the Lord be with you." 1 Samuel 17:36-37, NIV

There are things that come our way which will either destroy us or define us. Waiting is one of those things. If we want to win while waiting for God's promises to come to pass, we must

> remember the victories of our past when we are faced with the challenges of our present.

Make a list of the victories. Mark down the blessings in your life. When I thank God that I have a loaf of bread, I am less prone to notice I do not have butter. With this attitude, I can find amazing things to do with what I have instead of wishing for what I do not. God makes up the difference. What we celebrate attracts more of the same into our life. When He sees that we can celebrate Him even when we are in a position of need, He comes to our aid. For our soul to stay strong it is good to rehearse the goodness of God.

- Remembering helps us obey God's Word when we want to give up. (Psalm 119:55)
- Remembering reminds us God is Supreme. (Isaiah46:9)
- Remembering brings God's power to the forefront. (Deut. 7:17-18)

In the space between now and then, fill the gaps with tales of His deliverance. Tell your heart that God is faithful. Think again about the odds you have already defeated. Recognize that in some ways you are further along than you ever were. Find the good. Bless God for what you have right now. Gird yourself with gratitude and watch your spirit swell with joy. Once that joy comes, your strength will increase.

Participate

One of the slick tricks of the in-between is indifference. We get so focused on what we are going through that we stop getting involved. I see this so often. When people are in a funk, they usually just want to be left alone to wallow in their whining. People say that it does not feel good to feel bad. That statement is not true. It feels good to nurse your wounds and play the victim. It is not profitable, and it gives you headaches instead of progress, but sulking feels good sometimes if you let it. Yet, it is such an inappropriate response to the in-between seasons.

> The devil would love nothing more than to isolate you and keep you doing less for God instead of more.

I notice that when people are offended, they begin to do stuff they normally would not do. You do not necessarily have to be offended with a person; you can be offended by a process. Moreover, if you are secretly mad at God about the route you are on, it begins to show up. Our pouting starts in the lame excuses we use to get less involved in His Kingdom. We use our kids, our jobs, our education, our marriage, our travel – all sorts of things – to step back when we should be stepping up. What I want to understand is how we do not go to our jobs and tell them we need to step back for those same reasons. You know why? Because our jobs mean more. Of course they do. Some of the foolishness we come to God with is so bizarre we would never have the guts to approach our bosses with that reasoning. Yet, friends, we begged God to get the job in the first place. Now there is no time to serve Him. No. As Christians, as believers who made Jesus Christ our Lord it is our purpose to serve Him. Yes, you and I have to work and we can be an example in our workplace. However, we also have a responsibility to help further His kingdom through service.

Serving is also known as actively waiting. *"But they that wait upon the LORD shall renew their strength; they shall mount up with wings as eagles; they shall run, and not be weary; and they shall walk, and not faint."* Isaiah 40:31, KJV.

The word "wait" here means "to serve." While you and I are in limbo, we are to serve. Amazing things happen when we are busy doing the things of the Lord while waiting on a promise from Him.

Simeon in the New Testament had a promise from God. God had told him he would see the Messiah before he died. Luke 2 charts his story and describes him as "just and devout." The Spirit of the Lord led him into the temple and, in his old age, he saw Jesus as a child. Simeon was found in church serving.

The same thing happened with Anna the prophetess, who was also very old. She was young when she lost her husband, but instead of pulling away from serving, she turned her heart even more toward being involved in the service of God as an intercessor. She also saw her promise come to pass.

It was while Paul and his team were serving God by spreading the gospel using their testimonies in Acts 16, that divine provision came to them through a businesswoman named Lydia.

When Samuel was serving God in the temple (1 Samuel 3), he received his call from God. He had been separated from his family at a young age. No matter how righteous a cause, this still would be a sacrifice. Yet, Samuel diligently served instead of sulking, and in doing so, he received his life direction and purpose.

Therefore, instead of changing your seat from up front to the back rows, stay put. Do not resign from serving in an area of ministry or slow down in your giving. This will only take you away from your community of faith and from participating in the process of faithfulness. This kind of behavior and

> **resignation only shows that you are allowing your circumstances to change your faith instead of letting faith change your circumstances.**

It indicates a level of immaturity and highlights the desire to serve yourself because when you resign in your heart you become critical of everything around you.

During *the space between moments*, we must actively wait upon God. Until new instructions are given, follow the ones you already have. You know to serve others. You know to worship. You know to pray. You know to obey Him. Until your change comes, do these things wholeheartedly.

Practical Application

We should live a lifestyle of worship! If we fix our hearts, our thoughts, and our gaze on the absolute wonder of who God is, then faith, patience, and gratefulness will follow. There is nothing, absolutely nothing that can infuse strength into our souls during the in-between like worshiping God.

Consider It

Do you have a worship routine? If not, try this one:

Praise songs (10 mins)

Prayer exalting God (3 mins)

Prayer for others (3 mins)

Pray for leaders (2 mins)

Prayer of surrendering your day, issues, heart (5 mins)

Read a devotional (find some at pastorsara.com)(5mins)

Declare God's word over your day (2 mins)

List three worship songs you love:

1. ____________________

2. ____________________

3. ____________________

Internalize It

Meditate on and memorize this scripture:

O Lord, I will honor and praise your name, for you are my God. You do such wonderful things! You planned them long ago, and now you have accomplished them. Isaiah 25:1, NLT

Speak It

"Lord, You are great and worthy of all my worship and praise. I lift my eyes to you and believe that You are who You say You are. I lift my voice to You and thank You for saving my soul and for giving me a hope, a purpose, and a future. How good You are, God. Truly there is no one like You!"

Apply It

An attitude of gratitude changes your outlook on everything.

Be anxious for nothing, but in everything by prayer and supplication, ***with thanksgiving****, let your requests be made known to God; 7 and the peace of God, which surpasses all understanding, will guard your hearts and minds through Christ Jesus.* Philippians 4:6-7, NKJV

Seven

Work it Out

My daughter Heaven did me a favor once – she ran track and field. An avid soccer player who had the privilege of playing for some of the nation's top clubs, she was a scoring forward on all of her teams. She was fast and her start was incredibly quick. In fact, she was one of the quickest, if not the quickest girl in her age bracket and location at any given time. She ran with such passion and persistence. Her game face was one to rival. She left many defenders trailing. She was such a speedy torpedo with a soccer ball, I could just imagine how much faster she could be without one. I thought she would be amazing running track.

Well, to my surprise, she hated track and field. Imagine that. Be still my shocked heart. Logically, I figured since she played soccer and ran in the Texas heat, running track would be a breeze. Her long legs are built to run like a gazelle on the prairie – sincerely, it is a gorgeous sight watching her stride. It would be so easy for her to thrive in track and field, not to mention college scholarship (ka-ching)! I begged her to run year after year, but to no avail. She just wanted to play soccer.

Truth be told, I have leg envy, and wanted to vicariously live my track and field dreams through her. It stands to reason, if you have legs like a giraffe, you should run like a cheetah! "Just run for one season," I pleaded, "and my life will be complete, I can go to heaven in peace."

Ok, so maybe I was slightly exaggerating. However, this was my request, albeit a dramatic one.

Well, we finally came to a new season, a new year, and my annual pleading was about to pay off. Hope was on the horizon, my friends.

(Heaven with her Coach, USA Olympian John Drummond)

It was 2012 and Heaven had transferred as an eighth-grader to a new small school. To our surprise, there was a coach named Cedric she had known in the past, and he kept encouraging her to join the track team under Olympian Coach John Drummond. She resisted for all of 2012 while continuing to play soccer, basketball, and volleyball. Nevertheless, in 2013, something shifted. After bribing, threatening, and all but forcing her, she decided to run one season for me. I was ecstatic. She was skeptical. I was planning "mother of the Champ" speeches. She had no words. Not fully confident of what lay ahead for her as a track girl, Heaven contemplated what the process would be like, because honestly, she does that sort of thing – contemplate, brood, think, excessively plan. She is the kind of girl who weighs the pros and cons of a scenario, and in this case, she was really coming up short. Daily 2-3 hour practices, constant drills, a coach that required 100% every day, every time, in addition to her heavy dislike for running.

Heaven was just not feeling it…until…

Until she got a promise. A family friend of ours, who had been an incredible blessing in our lives, made her a promise: "Heaven, go out there and win. I promise, if you bring back a gold medal, I will do something for you that will blow your mind." After that, everything changed. She was motivated not by my years of pleading, but by this sudden promise. You see, this friend had a history of doing amazing things, so Heaven knew he had the ability to fulfill the promise he had made. She believed what he said, though she had no idea what "blow your mind" actually meant. It was a promise she held onto based on this man's previously proven integrity. Her imagination began to pulse with vivid scenes of how her mind could be blown. As her parent, I honestly could not fathom how one would blow the mind of a child who sees herself building a school for girls on every habitable continent. Her small dreams make my big ones quake. I thought, oh boy, this better be good.

Heaven had never done track for more than a week prior to this promise. She had no experience, only an expectation. She had an assignment to win at something in which she had not ever properly attempted. In my calculation, this was a recipe for disappointment and disaster. Do not get me wrong, I supported and believed in her. I believed she would make her best effort, but without any prior experience, could she really pull off winning gold medals? Even with those legs, could she hold her own against people who had been running for years? While she planned her triumph, I secretly planned for the tears of consolation. I mean, coming third could work for a first attempt, but GOLD? That would take years. Listen, I knew she was gifted, but truly thought my mother-of-the-golden-gazelle speeches would come after she had trained for a few seasons. I prepped for the "you did your best" chat instead. As a swimmer, it took me years in high school to get a gold medal. So this all seemed a bit unattainable, and had it been me, I would have just broken down and cried. But, it was not me…it was Heaven. She began to chomp on that promise like a bulldog with a bone.

The rubber was about to meet the road.

What was she really made of? We were about to find out! As her mom, I wanted to rescue her, eliminate the tough stuff, protect her from falling, and certainly from failing. I wanted to save her from disappointment, protect her from embarrassment, and shield her from the payment a dream requires from you. Nonetheless, she already believed. Her imagination had been whet by hopes and dreams. She saw the end, though not clearly, and she just knew it was for her good and would do her good. She knew the first step: She would have to show up and try out. Was the promise too big for her potential? Was the process too grueling for her determination? We all waited to see.

The Work

God says it this way in Ephesians 3:20: *"Now unto him that is able to do exceeding abundantly above all that we ask or think, according to the power that worketh in us…" (KJV) and again in 1 Corinthians 2:9 "But as it is written, Eye hath not seen, nor ear heard, neither have entered into the heart of man, the things which God hath prepared for them that love him." (KJV)*

This "blow-our-minds" kind of promise gives birth to desire, but desire without discipline is destructive and sets the path for personal disappointment.

> God clearly has great and amazing, out-of-this-world, bigger-than-big plans for us.

We get excited about the promise, and we should. We print it out, talk about it, dream about it, share it, and even believe it, but until we actually do something, the promise simply remains in the "believe" state. **Faith requires action**. Inactive faith is dead faith (see James 2:20).

Let me lay this out for you. God gives us a promise or we have a desire that lines up with His word. We want to see it come to pass. It can be a promotion, a new relationship, a personal best, a new business, a desire to be a missionary, or a great idea. Whatever it is, we see the end result in our minds, and we believe God will follow through. We know if we complain and have negative attitudes, it only slows us down, while having a hope anchored in faith, worship, obedience, and gratitude advances us. These things are all true, but they do not exempt us from the process of patience.

God is after our whole heart, and through this process of patience, we find out which pieces of our hearts still need to be captured by Him. And frankly, the only way to create true surrender is to endure an element of suffering. Every promise has a touch of tension.

Heaven was capable, but she had not been put under pressure yet. She was ready to go, but she was not trained. She was confident, but she was not cautious. She was about to go through what we call "the pressing." In this book its called the waiting. That span of development needed to create a person ready for the promise. I could only cover my eyes and pray the child would survive.

With pep in her step and a song on her lips, Heaven's zeal propelled her to the first day of practice. With every sprint she gave it her all. She did not pace herself and ran with her whole heart, not knowing there were 20 more sprints to do. At the first sign of stress, of unfamiliarity, and of struggle, what did she do? She threw up, but she did not give up. Overworked and underprepared, she bolted through the exercises, but she did not temper herself. She lacked the key element of pace and got winded, sick, and fatigued. In trying to impress the coach and others with her ability she imploded. Running her practice in haste showed her immaturity and inexperience. She was not conditioned for the process, she was only convinced of the promise.

> God is not just concerned with doing something for us and through us; He is also incredibly concerned with doing something in us.

There was an internal lesson Heaven was about to learn which would eventually help her on and off the track. These mini-setbacks of throwing up and being exhausted served as clues to the truth that she was missing something. However, it was up to her to see them as clues and not as a conclusion that she was not capable of winning.

I find we all do this sometimes. Here is an example: I may feel that God wants me to go to India. I envision the people there and the ministry I will do. The lives changed and the joy on people's faces, in my dream, become my heart's reward. If you left it up to me, I would pack my bags, buy a ticket, and get on the plane, arriving at the Shivaji Airport in Mumbai. Then, in all my excitement, I would go to the immigration line. Ready to launch out into the deep and reach all the beautiful children from my dream, I can see it, I can smell the wafts of curry-laden adventures…and then…embarrassment. What? I need a visa? Are you kidding me? Nope. Not a joke. If I am going to fulfill the dream, I actually, by law, need a visa and a work permit to live and serve in India.

Just because God says "Go!" it does not mean right now. There is a maturation process that has to take place while waiting. Considering where I was going in my dream, I would need to think about and prepare many things: accommodation, relationships, entry requirements, vaccinations, target groups, fundraising, length of ministry, dietary concerns, and so on. An obtained promise without proper preparation is like building a house on a foundation that is too small. The plan can be spectacular, but it will not be sustainable.

> The only thing I have experienced that is worse than waiting on God, is not waiting on Him.

My impatience always costs me more than I am willing to pay, and instead of bringing me closer to seeing my dreams come true, it keeps me further away.

Sacrifice

When I watched Heaven during this season of her life, she taught me the final keys to waiting effectively. I realized we must have a why that is bigger than our where, meaning,

> our reason for continuing must be greater than our present situation.

Looking at Heaven, I finally understood some of the gaps I had created in my own waiting experiences. I saw what I had not grasped previously: In order to succeed in receiving the promises of God, there are two things we cannot get away from - *sacrifice* and *surrender*.

One meaning of the word sacrifice is "the surrender or destruction of something prized or desirable for the sake of something considered as having a higher or more pressing claim." [2] Sacrifice is the segue to the supernatural occurring in our lives. When we are willing to give up what is most precious to us for something that is valuable to God, He is moved.

---

2 http://www.dictionary.com/browse/sacrifice?s=t

This is one of the most important manifestations of our faith and belief in God – the act of sacrifice. It is a decider. It helps us determine what is most important. It locates the value system in our hearts. It causes us to ask the hard questions…How much do we really value God, His principles, and His promises? Is God truly most important in our lives, our loves, our comforts, our habits, our pleasures, our friendships, our jobs, our desires, and our families? Sacrifice is the blade that cuts away hypocrisy in our hearts. Our words say, "God, You are first," but our works may tell another tale. We must own the fact that, oftentimes for us, being comfortable trumps being committed to His process. Yet, it is only through sacrifice that we can really excel in God.

In the end, Heaven did excel. In her first, last and only season of running track, she won seven gold medals two silvers and one bronze. She was the MVP athlete of the year. She won medals in 100m, 200m, 400m and long jump. That year she happened to be the only 8th grade female participant for her school. Her incredible performance singlehandedly gained the scores needed for her school to place second in Regionals. She won numerous awards and accolades. She gained personal pride and realized she could go further than she ever imagined. It came at a price with a coach who pushed her relentlessly but she was willing to pay the price because of the prize that was promised.

The Sacrifice of Time

One of the most important things we need to sacrifice to the Lord is our time. Spending valuable time with God establishes Him as Lord and Master. The more time we spend in His presence, the better understanding we have of who He is, of what His desires are, and of the plans He has for us. Spending time to worship and know God is the first of all sacrifices to make in the life of the believer, and during the period of waiting, it often is the one that is most threatened. The devil wants to separate us from God, so he speaks lies to us, sends situations to trip us up, and puts thoughts in our minds to cause us to question God's love, faithfulness, and ability. If we separate ourselves from Christ, who is our Life Source, our faith wanes. Our confidence grows weaker the longer we are away from the presence of God. Doubt creeps in, and before we know it, we shrink back in defeat, all because we did not make spending time with the Lord a priority.

The Bible is so clear about the importance of spending time with God. We think we can just schedule Him in on our drive to work, while we are in the shower, when we are walking on the treadmill, or running a mile. We have Him in the background playing through our homes while we clean or shave. Nevertheless, this is not concentrated, sacrificial time; this is "I did some spiritual penance for the day to clear my conscience and do my Christian duty" time. No, sacrifice means putting Him first and making concentrated, intentional efforts to speak to Him, praise Him, listen to Him, and pour our hearts out to Him.

Here are some scriptures on which to meditate regarding making God our first priority in life:

1. "Love the Lord your God with all your heart and with all your soul and with all your mind." Matthew 22:37, NIV

2. "And God spoke all these words, saying, "I am the Lord your God, who brought you out of the land of Egypt, out of the house of slavery. You shall have no other gods before me." Exodus 20:1-3, NIV

3. Then Jesus said to him, "Be gone, Satan! For it is written, 'You shall worship the Lord your God and him only shall you serve.'" Matthew 4:10, ESV

4. Include the following in your time. I gave a suggested schedule in Chapter 6 but this is so important I am saying it again differently:

a. Praise & worship – The act of speaking or singing words of affection and adoration regarding God's person and His power.

b. Thanksgiving – Celebrating God for what He has done.

c. Prayer – Pouring out your requests, your complaints, your heartbreak, and your joys.

d. Reading – Taking a moment to read the Bible. Select a verse or principle to meditate on throughout the day.

e. Listening – Pausing long enough to ask God to speak to your spirit and waiting to hear what He has to say.

f. Journal – take a notebook or electronic app to reflect on your time with the Lord.

Begin with small amounts of time. You may allot 2-5 minutes to each item and increase as you go. Your time with God is personal and special. This guideline can help you maximize your time with God. Maybe spend some time worshipping in the morning, then on your lunch break read and pray for others, and then before bed, listen for His voice. The point is to sacrifice your time as a signal to God that your priority is Him in all things.

The Sacrifice of Praise

Praise reflects what is in our hearts. It reveals where our affections lie. Whatever we praise, we respect. Whatever we respect, we receive from. Whatever we receive from, we respond toward. Whatever we respond toward, we emulate. Whatever we emulate, we are rewarded with. So you see, praise is the first action in a series of actions that sets in motion a reward.

David was described by God as *"a man after mine own heart, which shall fulfil all my will."* (Acts 13:22b, KJV) What an honor to be noted by

God like this. We know David was not a perfect person. He had committed adultery and murder. How could God still regard David so highly when he had failed so miserably? The answer is simple: In all of David's ways, He always came back to God. He was a worshipper, and whenever he was wrong, he ran toward God and not away from Him. Psalm 145 really gives an idea of how David praised and how He saw God's heart. It shows us how he trusted Him. This Psalm is a great pattern for us to emulate:

I will exalt you, my God and King,

and praise your name forever and ever.

I will praise you every day;

yes, I will praise you forever.

Great is the Lord! He is most worthy of praise!

No one can measure his greatness.

Let each generation tell its children of your mighty acts;

let them proclaim your power.

I will meditate on your majestic, glorious splendor

and your wonderful miracles.

Your awe-inspiring deeds will be on every tongue;

I will proclaim your greatness.

Everyone will share the story of your wonderful goodness;

they will sing with joy about your righteousness.

The Lord is merciful and compassionate,

slow to get angry and filled with unfailing love.

The Lord is good to everyone.

He showers compassion on all his creation.

All of your works will thank you, Lord,

and your faithful followers will praise you.

They will speak of the glory of your kingdom;

they will give examples of your power.

They will tell about your mighty deeds

and about the majesty and glory of your reign.

For your kingdom is an everlasting kingdom.

You rule throughout all generations.

The Lord always keeps his promises;

he is gracious in all he does.

The Lord helps the fallen

and lifts those bent beneath their loads.

The eyes of all look to you in hope;

you give them their food as they need it.

When you open your hand,

you satisfy the hunger and thirst of every living thing.

The Lord is righteous in everything he does;

he is filled with kindness.

The Lord is close to all who call on him,

yes, to all who call on him in truth.

He grants the desires of those who fear him;

he hears their cries for help and rescues them.

The Lord protects all those who love him,

but he destroys the wicked.

I will praise the Lord,

and may everyone on earth bless his holy name

forever and ever. Psalm 145, NLT

(You can download my message, "At the Core – A Look at the Heart of David" at http://wotfc.com/sermons/01475-the-core)

The Sacrifice of Treasure

The next thing we must be willing to sacrifice is our treasure. Unfortunately, people are often turned off when we talk about treasure or money. The principles of God cannot be overlooked because of the poor decisions of a few people who mismanaged or mishandled finances in the kingdom.

> Just because a principle has been violated or abused does not mean it does not work or that it ceases to exist.

yesterday, today, and forever, His principles do not change, even if people have brought shame to them.

Sacrifice in our finances is important. Please do not throw this book down now and hang me out to dry. Hear me out a sec, because I live this kind of life. I endured times of true poverty growing up. Hurricanes devastated our country and left us without water and electricity for weeks. Finding food could be difficult, and sometimes we were left to eat cans of corned beef heated over a coal stove. At other times, since my mother was absent from my life due to drugs and my father was away for months at a time due to work, we had to fend for ourselves making the best of a head of cabbage and some carrots. I do not want you to think I am some fraudulent person trying to rip you off of your hard-earned cash. I have been without running water, electricity, lunch money and would steal little bags of banana chips from the store. I have also had plenty. My increase is definitely linked to my sacrifice in this area. Truly, I've had many games played on me and I've ran games. At this point the lying, deceiving, foolish person I used to be doesn't exist anymore. I am not about that life. I am honestly putting it out there to let you know, I am a person who has seen the power of sacrifice and the increase it brings.

You see, most people think that God's biggest competition is the devil. Actually, it could be money. The devil is already defeated. But that money? Well, it becomes an idol in our life. An idol we will spend all our hours running after. This is why Matthew 6:24 calls money a master and warns us that we cannot serve two masters at the same time: "No man can serve two masters: for either he will hate the one, and love the other; or else he will hold to the one, and despise the other. Ye cannot serve God and mammon." (KJV) Verse 21 of this same chapter says, *"For where your treasure is there will your heart be also."* (KJV)

> Whatever you invest in becomes your priority.

That is why financial sacrifice is really not about money; financial sacrifice is about dethroning the love of money for the love of God.

Financial provision for the Christian believer is tied to God's view of treasure. Your dreams cost money. The Kingdom of God needs financial support to advance. You can start a business, but you need money to run it. God can fulfill His promise and you can get pregnant, but you need to be able to pay for diapers. So, you see, some of our promises have a financial need attached. This being the case, we cannot ignore that there is a financial sacrifice involved in the promise as well.

> The cure for greed is generosity.

A heart that is generous creates hands that give. Hands that give, express the core heart of God, which is generous love.

There is financial obedience and there is financial sacrifice. Financial obedience is based on God's preset criteria. This is where we come into alignment with what He has already decided. Financial sacrifice, while sometimes prompted by God, is set by our own will. To put ourselves in the best position possible while waiting on God, we need to be in full obedience to all that we know of Him. Then we can truly say we have "done all to stand" (see Ephesians 6:13), for we can have full confidence that we have followed Him and that our promise is on its way. The only hindrance will be an act of disobedience. As with many things, there is a way to be obedient to God with our finances. He has a standard.

The Standard. Have you ever bought a shirt or a piece of clothing and seen a little sticker with a number on it? That sticker is a quality control number to let the manufacturer know who inspected the garment. If the garment is damaged, the manufacturer can track down who violated the standard during inspection. The garment is no good if it is made wrong. The same goes with the kingdom. God has a required standard for the believer called "tithe and offering." It is a standard created to make you believe in God rather than money.

Will a man rob God? Yet ye have robbed me. But ye say, Wherein have we robbed thee? In tithes and offerings. Malachi 3:8, KJV

God has grouped these two together: tithe and offering. The tithe is a set ten percent, but the offering is based on your own decision.

But this I say, He which soweth sparingly shall reap also sparingly; and he which soweth bountifully shall reap also bountifully. Every man according as he purposeth in his heart, so let him give; not grudgingly, or of necessity: for God loveth a cheerful giver. 2 Corinthians 9:6-7, KJV

Financial obedience has rewards. We obey God because we love Him, but as a good Father, He also rewards those who obey. It is not wrong to appreciate and anticipate the rewards of God when He sets them in front of us. The reward for obeying the standard of tithe and offering is seen in the following verses.

Bring ye all the tithes into the storehouse, that there may be meat in mine house, and prove me now herewith, saith the LORD of hosts, if I will not open you the windows of heaven, and pour you out a blessing, that there shall not be room enough to receive it. And I will rebuke the devourer for your sakes, and he shall not destroy the fruits of your ground; neither shall your vine cast her fruit before the time in the field, saith the LORD of hosts. Malachi 3:10-11, KJV

And God is able to make all grace abound toward you; that ye, always having all sufficiency in all things, may abound to every good work. 2 Corinthians 9:8, KJV

> There are promises assigned to principles.

On the most basic level, obeying God with your finances helps you resist the money temptations along the way.

Sow a Seed. Some people give jewelry, cars, or an item of great value as a financial seed. Sometimes it is unplanned and sacrificial. I remember when we believed God for our son. Like I told you, God had to do a work in my heart because my faith was clouded by doubt, jealousy, and envy. Going into the third doctor's office, I was excited and apprehensive at the same time… excited because his reputation for solving infertility issues was renowned (I truly had higher hopes in him than in God), and apprehensive because he was about to discuss our results. I did not want to be let down again or hear another report labeling me infertile and unproductive or telling me that achieving a pregnancy was impossible or futile. We walked into his office and sat across from him at his desk. Hand to heart, the conversation went like this:

"Hi Mr. and Mrs. Conner, I have the results of your tests, and our findings are the same as the previous doctors'. The mobility of the sperm is very low, and they are not very viable now. What we could do is try a procedure called ICSI, whereby we place one sperm directly into the egg, which we would need to harvest. There's no guarantee this would work, due to the low mobility of the sperm, but outside of donor sperm (insert my shock and awe) this would be the best option. However, some people still choose not to do it."

My husband chimed in, "Well, doc, that sounds good. By the way, why would people not do it? You said it is not guaranteed, is that it?"

"Well, usually it is due to the cost."

"What's the cost?"

"$9,600 per try but it could take more than one."

I was not bothered by this. I reasoned to myself that if someone I loved was in jail, I would find the bail money. Hence, let us pawn all our stuff, get a home equity loan, sell all our goods, live a nomadic life, I didn't care, do whatever it takes. Yes, let us do this. But then I zoned back in the conversation and heard my husband saying…

"$9,600? Well, doc, let me say it like this…you said it is not a guaranteed procedure, right? I am gonna tell you what, I am gonna do. I am gonna take a chance with God. I am gonna give God that money, and my faith will see you on the other side. Sweet let's go."

No. Sweet is not going anywhere. Then he got up to leave. I am certain I began to almost cuss in my mind. What the Hades? Take a chance on God? Sow a $10,000 seed somewhere else and just believe? I could not process it. I wanted to go with the doctor's option, truth be told. I would have found that money for the doctor but to find it to take a chance with God? Hmmph. I pouted. I shut ***all*** the way down. I muttered to myself like a sourpuss all the way home because I did not get my own way. I felt deflated and defeated.

I walked into our home with a dark cloud over my head, and my husband told me to go into the bathroom and pray until I believed. First of all, I was already irritated and felt he was a dream killer. So, I honestly didn't want to hear a thing he was saying to me. Now, he is bossing me around and telling me to go and pray? What does he think I have been doing all these years? I was so piping hot! I knew he was right, but man, I just wanted to be right in my wrong for a second. But I unwillingly did what he told me to do. I came out of the bathroom a couple of hours later looking like a beat-up boxer with puffy eyes and a red nose. But in my heart, I had resolve. I would believe God. I would be in agreement and sow this significant sacrificial seed. We would bank it all on God and wait patiently.

In the third week of October 2008 we sowed that seed of $10,000 at a conference at New Light Church in Houston. As Bishop Hilliard was closing his message, his wife, Pastor Bridget, felt a prophetic push from God to pray for people who wanted to get pregnant. A few couples went up. I will never forget it. Our heart's desire was noticed by God and being announced in public, moments after we had given a sacrificial seed.

You see, I would have found that money if my kid was in jail, if my dad needed surgery, if my house was in foreclosure, or my husband was in trouble. We find what we want to find when it is important to us. Having this baby was important, and we took a leap of faith and nearly emptied our accounts in gathering this seed.

January 2009 came, and it was time for our annual church fast. Since I take fasting seriously, I knew I was about to put my body through some rigor. The thought came to me to take a pregnancy test to make sure I was still NOT pregnant so I could go fully into the fast. I bought a test and took it. Two solid lines…I was pregnant!! I could not believe it. Let me rephrase. I did not believe it. My daughter and husband were running around the house cheering, dancing, and praising God, but in my heart I was hoping this was not some tumor showing up as a pregnancy. I did not rejoice. I know you just want to slap me right now! After all this praying and believing, my promise was right there and I could not receive it.

Bright and early the next morning, I took another test, and the results were the same: PREGNANT! I called my doctor and asked if two tests could be wrong. She said, "Sara, you are pregnant; come into my office ASAP." When I went in, I realized I had conceived a month to the week after we had sown that sacrificial seed. We truly believe that act of faith demonstrated our deep desire and our trust in God. Our sacrifice got God's attention and set us up for the supernatural to take place. It showed we were in agreement with believing Him over the doctors, and we were willing to be obedient to His Spirit. We had both felt the leading of the Lord to sow that amount during that conference. It was a defining moment for our faith, and we decided to jump into believing with both feet. Landon was born on August 25, 2009, full-term plus a few days. You saw his cute face earlier. This is a recorded miracle. My doctor is recorded on video stating this is against the medical evidence.

> Miracles happen when we sacrifice.

Sacrifice is part of the process of waiting.

Believing Despite the Odds

Landon came out with his robust, juicy self, weighing just under nine pounds – imagine that! Abundance already. The very first night, he began to shake, and the nurses asked me if I had gestational diabetes. I did not, but he was responding like a child who needed insulin. I started to panic. Right after that, he failed the hearing test. Yes people, within 24 hours I saw my promise sent to the NICU, and my blood pressure shot up the wazoo while I tried to locate the seeds of faith in my heart. "Steady Freddy" Eben, my husband, was not fazed by this nightmare. He began to say, "God has not brought us this far to leave us now. Whatever he has begun in us, He is faithful to complete it." I got a bed in the NICU. They needed me to begin nursing as soon as possible. Everything was swirling around in my mind. "Can you test him again on his hearing?" I asked as I prayed. They retested him, and he passed. I began to nurse and he stabilized, allowing us to leave the NICU after a few days. After that we went to the pediatrician a few weeks later and she believed he had hip dysplasia. Savior Divine! What in the world was that? His hips were clicking, so she thought he may need to wear a brace. His bones probably were not set properly, etc., etc.…on and on she went.

I took Landon to see a specialist, and she confirmed he had some clicking in his hips, but she doubted the pediatrician's diagnosis. She would keep an eye on him for a year, just in case. A year went by and Landon was cleared. Absolutely no hip problems. No health problems at all. All was well, praise God!

We believe the sacrificial seed we sowed carried on over into Landon's life. We believe it lived on in his future. When you get a watermelon and bust it open you see hundreds if not thousands of seeds, correct? Yet how many seeds do you actually need to plant to reap watermelons? Just one. That one seed has many harvests attached to it. There are seeds within the seed, forests within the tree, and vines of melons within the first planted sacrifice. This is the power of a sacrificial seed sown.

The Shunammite Woman

Sacrificial seeds are displayed for us many times in the Bible. I have to encourage you because you may have sown seed. You may have sacrificed. The devil and other people may mock your giving. They taunt your commitment and plant seeds of regret in your heart. I have come to announce to you that

> God is not forgetful of your sacrifice.

Come with me to explore the account in 2 Kings 4 where the Prophet Elisha and a Shunammite woman have a powerful encounter, all because of a sacrificial seed. Grab your pen, Bible, and notebook… you are going to love this.

This story takes place in the small village of Shunem, which belongs to the tribe of Issachar. Elisha passes through this town every now and then, and eventually gets noticed by a woman of great standing. Compassion fills her heart toward Elisha, and she speaks to her husband about making a sacrifice. She tells her husband she wants to build a room for Elisha to stay in when he passes through. Together they built a room or apartment where the prophet could rest and be refreshed.

This significant seed created a turnaround in this woman's life. Honoring the messenger of God to this degree caught the attention of God. The Shunammite woman did not know it at the time, but her season of fulfillment sped up and her waiting time shortened. You see, this woman had a secret desire, something that only God would know about and only God could bring to pass. For years she had this desire burning inside of her. She probably prayed about it, worried about it, and cried about it. Her desire had stayed the same for years, but this year, her sacrifice made the difference.

This woman's desire was to have a son. It was a dream that lay dormant in her heart, one she hoped to have fulfilled, but waiting on it to happen was wearing her out. She was disappointed and eventually just learned to live with the unfulfilled dream. She lowered her expectations and concluded that maybe she was not meant to have a child. But, that sacrifice she made? It brought a return. She housed the man of God, a carrier of God's word, and in return, the Word of God came back to her. Let us read the story together:

One day Elisha went to the town of Shunem. A wealthy woman lived there, and she urged him to come to her home for a meal. After that, whenever he passed that way, he would stop there for something to eat.

She said to her husband, "I am sure this man who stops in from time to time is a holy man of God. Let's build a small room for him on the roof and furnish it with a bed, a table, a chair, and a lamp. Then he will have a place to stay whenever he comes by."

One day Elisha returned to Shunem, and he went up to this upper room to rest. He said to his servant Gehazi, "Tell the woman from Shunem I want to speak to her." When she appeared, Elisha said to Gehazi, "Tell her, 'We appreciate the kind concern you have shown us. What can we do for you? Can we put in a good word for you to the king or to the commander of the army?'"

"No," she replied, "my family takes good care of me."

Later Elisha asked Gehazi, "What can we do for her?"

Gehazi replied, "She does not have a son, and her husband is an old man."

"Call her back again," Elisha told him. When the woman returned, Elisha said to her as she stood in the doorway, "Next year at this time you will be holding a son in your arms!"

"No, my lord!" she cried. "O man of God, do not deceive me and get my hopes up like that."

But sure enough, the woman soon became pregnant. And at that time the following year she had a son, just as Elisha had said. 2 Kings 4:8-17, NLT

After this, the story takes an unexpected turn. Some time passed, and then the Shunammite woman's son had a headache and suddenly died. Scrambling for hope and an answer, she placed the boy upon Elisha's bed. I want you to get this. She placed her promise on her sacrifice, reminding herself that the seed she had sown in sacrifice needed to respond now in this time of sorrow. You can allow your sacrifice to speak up for you; it can remind God of His promises. That is exactly what this woman did. She went back to the place of her greatest seed. Grabbing a servant and with pandemonium beating down the doors of her heart, she rushed to find Elisha. As a mother, she felt the jaws of darkness closing in over the light of her life. Her mind filled with memories of holding her son and hearing him laugh, even as it fought the image of the cold, stiff body she had left in the prophet's chamber.

Elisha sees her approaching from a distance and wonders what her haste is all about. Concerned, he asks his servant to meet her and see what could be so pressing. This woman was truly remarkable. When the servant asked about her son, she declared that all was well. But once she got into Elisha's presence, she broke down. Grabbing his feet, her grief poured out like a tumultuous rain. Her soul was overwhelmed, and her heart was broken. Elisha went with her and found the child dead upon his bed. Moments later, the child was resurrected and reunited with his mother.

We have to understand

> a sacrifice lives beyond the moment in which it is given.

It is something that protects the promise and continues reproducing a harvest in our future. When we wait on God, sacrifices are often required. Sacrifice is a language of Heaven. God understands sacrifices.

He who did not spare his own Son, but gave him up for us all - how will he not also, along with him, graciously give us all things?" Romans 8:32, NIV

For Something Greater

God understands the concept of giving up what you love most for something greater. In sacrificing Jesus, His one and only Son, He gained many sons.

The space between here and there is often filled with sacrifices. We must be willing to risk it all to have it all. Great men and women in the Bible show us that sacrifice is inevitable…

Abraham sacrificed his home by obeying God to go to another place, even though God did not let Abraham in on the secret of exactly where He was sending him.

Mary the mother of Jesus sacrificed her reputation to be obedient to God.

Peter the apostle sacrificed his career to follow Jesus.

We see that

> a sacrificial seed evokes a response from God.

In 2 Chronicles 1:6-7, Solomon sacrificed 1,000 burnt offerings to God, and that same night God asked Solomon, "What do you want? Ask and I will give it to you." There was no waiting period. God shifted Solomon's life immediately after he made a sacrifice.

Then there is the widow in 1 Kings 17. There was a severe famine and she and her son were down to their last meal. In her mind, this was the end. It was a hopeless situation, and she was out of options. Elijah told her to sacrifice the last of what she had. Even though it was a crazy request, she obeyed, and instantly her season of waiting changed. A miracle took place. The seed she gave multiplied and continued to bring a harvest for days and days, helping her sustain herself and her son through the season of famine.

Surrender

> On the other side of the coin of sacrifice is a heart of surrender.

Nothing matters if our hearts are not surrendered to God. The Holy Spirit wants to give us instructions, visions, dreams, and strategies. Our spirits long for words of wisdom and love. A yielded heart will listen. A yielded heart seeks the path God takes and joins Him on the journey. A heart that is pliable is one that partners with God. Though the flesh cries for its own way and comfort beckons, the person fully surrendered will be also be fully committed to obeying God, no matter what. A person like that is unstoppable.

"If you love Me, keep My commandments." John 14:15, NKJV

Obeying God is evidence that we love Him. We have to make up our minds to obey the will of God at all costs. We cannot afford to hinder our own progress in God with disobedience. Seriously. There are times my heart is fully surrendered, when my will is set in agreement to obey His Word – the revealed Word and the Word spoken to my heart. In these times, no matter what comes against me, I am full of peace and confidence. It is hard to shake my faith and trust in God. It is as if I am encapsulated. Worry and stress do not have a chance.

Sometimes, however, comfort can become an enemy to my faith. Being a slave to my routine or being happy in the familiar ways of my everyday life can leave me indifferent to the instructions of God. Then I become anxious, that nagging little feeling caused by disobedience makes me worry. I lose composure, and instead of relying on God, I get stuck in the rut of sameness. When we let what we know rule our lives, things get boring. Truly. No zest, no flavor, just predictable rhythms. We know there is something more, but we just cannot quite get to it because we hold on – we hold onto our past, to what is familiar, and to what we know. We get scared of risk and therefore become scarred by the results of our stagnation. As children of God we must go to a deeper place in Him. It is there in the seat of full surrender, and not in the chair of stubbornness, that we accelerate our progress.

Practical Application

We must ask ourselves hard questions to get to the root of our resistance for obedience. Only then can we truly get rid of the clutter that hinders our way forward. Here are some of these hard questions to get you started…

Consider It

Am I afraid to risk it all for God? Why?

____

____

____

____

What fears are holding me back? What can I do to move forward through these fears?

When God asks me to make a sacrifice, what is the first thought that comes to my mind?

Speak It

"Father, You have given me all I have, and all I have is Yours. Today I choose to lay down any rights that I have to my earthly possessions, time, or pleasure. I surrender fully to You and declare that my life is Yours and Yours alone. Help me not to be stingy. Help me to see that sacrifice could very well be the thing needed to bring to life the seed of promise that is lying dormant in my soul. Give me abundant faith and a deep assurance that You will perform the promise to completion. Hallelujah!"

Apply It

You may not know right away if you are supposed to sacrifice money, time, a gift or your talent and if you feel you should, you may not know yet where to sow that money seed. Trust God to reveal that to you. However, you do know that spending time with the King of the Universe on a daily basis is absolutely something you should sacrifice. That sacrifice can start immediately; that sacrifice can start today.

So humble yourselves before God. Resist the devil, and he will flee from you. Come close to God, and God will come close to you. Wash your hands, you sinners; purify your hearts, for your loyalty is divided between God and the world.
James 4:7-8, NLT

on the couch with a blanket and a cup of coffee. This time and this space should be sacred. To get you started and to keep you accountable, journal one thing that comes out of your conversation with God for the next 7 days:

Day 1

____

____

____

____

Day 2

____

____

____

____

Day 3

Day 4

Day 5

Day 6

Day 7

Eight

God is With Us

How could I believe in God? I asked myself that question so many times. Looking back over my life, I realized I had faced countless disappointments, and I really needed something and someone to believe in. As a young, misguided teenager, I did not understand the impact of drug addiction. Honestly, I did not know until some years later how addicted my mother really was to crack cocaine. I knew her fiery personality, her boisterous laughter, her hard discipline, and the vivacious fervency with which she lived her life. Her absences became normal to me, but they never made me feel any less disappointed.

Growing up under such extremes in life had bred a clawing uncertainty in my mind. I needed reliability, constancy, and an unfailing love that would see beauty in brokenness. It was during these broken, confused teenage years that I met Jesus. I had never heard much about Him before. I did not know that He had been broken, too. I had no idea that He had also been abandoned, looked down upon, and rejected. But when I found out, I knew that I understood Him, and He understood me. I saw reflected in His love an ability to crawl up out of my loneliness to a place of kindness I had never known. How could I refuse this invitation? I had to take the risk. I needed to know the wonder of it all.

For the first time, I was face-to-face with possibility. I will never forget it. Sitting in the back of a church auditorium. The lights dimmed just enough to hide my discomfort. The stiffness of the fabric itched my thigh as I tried to be at ease in my first-ever attempt to wear "church clothes." My friend did not tell me it would be like this. I felt so utterly stupid. Regretting accepting the invitation to attend this youth meeting at Church on the Rock Jamaica, I squirmed in my seat. Alone. In the back. Arguing with myself, I shouldn't have come. But how could I refuse my friend's invite? She hounded me week after week, begging me to just "try it," like it was a new pair of shoes or a flavor of ice cream. "What do you have to lose?" she asked, and in that instant, after a full summer of incessant pleading, I decided to go to the youth meeting.

There I was, and every familiar face I saw in the rows ahead of me served to corner me with shame. *Oh no, it is that girl from my school, the Christian girl who I laughed at for wearing her hair so weird. It still looks weird to me, but how could I have embarrassed her like that?* I was so afraid that all these girls might see me. I slid down further and further into my seat and hoped they would not notice me. I thought to myself, *Why is it so loud in here, and what is going on?*

I raised my eyes to see what my ears could not discern. Dancing. Arms in the sky. Who exactly were these people looking at up in the ceiling? They looked so happy. They looked so free. My mind was overwhelmed with all the problems I faced. It was only a few months before this that I had almost been gang raped when I ran away from home. I was worried that I might not get promoted to the next grade that year because I failed so many subjects not because of my intellect but because I lacked purpose. My palms began to sweat. Those stupid girls at our rival school had spread rumors about me. Would my Dad be back by Christmas? Had anyone seen my Mom? I wanted a different life. My breathing was getting shallow. I felt so alone. Why did I, one of the most popular girls in school, feel so alone? How were all these teenagers singing this funny music, so happy?

"Jesus Christ came and He died for your sins. It does not matter who you are. It does not matter if rumors are spread about you. For God so loved the world – meaning you! He loves you, He sent His only begotten Son into the world, and if you believe on Him, you will never perish but have eternal life."

I opened my eyes and found myself on my knees. Looking up from my place of despair, I saw a pair of the kindest brown eyes and a huge smile looking back at me. Debbie Keane held me in her arms at the altar of the first and most important sacrifice I would ever make. I felt so loved, and in that moment, under the voice of her husband Andrew, I gave my life to Christ. I had to believe in this God who loves me. And I still believe in His wonder.

My dreams grew as His love within me flourished. The more I understood Him, the less I underestimated Him.

> It was only a matter of time before I began to see the true magic of God.

The miracle we often miss is the one happening within us, and during that season, God began transforming me from the inside out. As we walked together, I learned His stride. As I spoke with Him, I adapted to His cadence. As I listened to Him, I heard his heartbeat echoed in my own.

I wanted to run out and conquer the world, and He wanted to conquer the worlds within me. He wanted to be my Champion, vanquishing every enemy of self-doubt, fearfulness and anguish. Knowing the seasons of waiting that would come in my future, He established in my heart a deep-rooted truth:

> **God is for me, with me, and in me – therefore, I am undefeatable.**

This is the truth that still holds me when I am in the valley, the one that comforts me when I am in the midst of the chaos of a trying season. It is the anchor during the storms and a lighthouse when I am losing my way. Learning to wait begins with waiting on Him. In serving God, we find out His preferences and the things that grieve His heart. We see how worship moves Him and how evil angers Him. We witness His awe as well as the awfulness that can happen because He has given us free will. We still hold the keys. We can choose to do it our way or believe Him enough to surrender to His way.

But he said to me, 'My grace is sufficient for you, for my power is made perfect in weakness.' Therefore I will boast all the more gladly about my weaknesses, so that Christ's power may rest on me. 2 Corinthians 12:9, NIV

I love that verse. His power is MADE perfect or mature in our weakness not in our rebellion. There is a wonderful thing God wants to do in our lives. Everyone admires a diamond because of its shine. Why is that? It is because we appreciate the process that was required to bring it to its final place of brilliance.

This process begins with mining. Deep within the surface of the earth, blasting, drilling, and digging, the search commences for raw diamonds. We can imagine that this is like the beginning stages of God birthing a dream in our hearts. His Spirit must move past all our borders, boundaries, pains, carnality, and humanity in order to mine out the seeds of promise for our lives. Nothing is obvious at this stage. It is all a bit dark and unknown. We know that something is going on inside of us. We feel a shift, a discomfort, as the seed of God begins to grate against our norm.

Then there is the crushing, the pressure required to fortify the diamond. We know there is a promise; we can even see the end with brilliance in mind. The weight of where we are seek to crush the hope of where we know we want to be. This is the beginning of walking through ***the space between***.

We must walk away from the familiar, from friends, and from old mindsets, and this can break our hearts. Surviving this crushing is dependent upon saturating ourselves in the presence of God and reminding ourselves of His promises.

At this point, the diamond still is not shiny. It is dull and brute, so it gets thrown into the third, and probably the most difficult, stage of its process – separation. Too many rocks pose as diamonds just as too many ideas pose themselves as inspiration from God. This is the lonely part of waiting – deciphering between your own thoughts and the thoughts of God. As you wait to hear the next instruction, people will often weigh in on your unfinished process, which can weigh down your spirit. Every step of the way, we have to understand that God never leaves us alone. The lie of the devil is that we are alone in this, and that simply is not true. From the miner to the cutter to the jeweler to the retailer,

> someone is always assigned to support you in this waiting process.

God has faith partners positioned along the way. You may feel especially lonely in this period of separation, but you are never alone, for God is with you in the valley, in the flood, on the mountain, in the desert, by the streams, on the highways, in the light, and in the dark. There is nowhere He cannot find you and no place He cannot reach you.

"Listen! The LORD's arm is not too weak to save you, nor is his ear too deaf to hear you call." Isaiah 59:1, NLT

Separation is not just a call to consecration, it is also setting down our agendas, purifying the motives of our hearts, drowning out the outward noises, and learning to love the hand that leads us through the most obscure of times. There is a battering and a bruising that can take place, yet we must know the diamond of our promise is built to overcome even this. For just as the diamond is the hardest gem in the world, so the promise of God is the most indestructible medium in the universe. After all, it is founded on the Word of God, and we know that "Heaven and earth will pass away but my words will never pass away." Matthew 24:35, NIV

As our promise – be it a spouse, a promotion, an increase, or a call – waits at the end, we are being fortified and must now enter the cutting stage. This gets rid of what separation failed to remove. Any tiny particles of flesh, selfishness, pride, narcissism, fear, bitterness, envy, comparison, failure, or regret must be sliced from our character with perfect precision. This journey of maturation moves us forward, and we are the only ones with the will to stop the process. We can quit. We can give in and give up. We can abort or we can press our way toward the finish line.

The most beautiful thing about the cutting of a diamond is that olive oil and water are used on its surface as it is being cut. I am floored by the beauty of God in this. In our most trying moments, the water of His Word and the oil of His Spirit work in harmony with each other to soothe, sustain, and sharpen us. As the Master Craftsman designs the facets, each new chisel testifies to what we have overcome in the dark, climbed through in the valley, and made it through in the loneliness. Every angle tells a story. Every bend celebrates a defining moment. In the palm of the craftsman, the diamond yields itself, fully surrendered. Like the diamond, after this process of waiting, you are now ready to SHINE. You are set in a place and are part of a piece that highlights your brilliance the most.

Shine!

Like a diamond, you and I are ready to massively bling when we near the light. You see, I learned that the art of waiting is understanding that I have the most clarity when my character is formed, my faith is tested, my maturity is molded, my sins are repented, my praise is perfected, and my heart is surrendered. The waiting exists to make sure we get rid of the dross and are drawn to the Light. As long as we stay close and allow Christ to shine through us, the promises of God, the dreams in our hearts, will beam throughout eternity. Others will be blessed, God will be glorified, and we will be fulfilled. This, my friends, is

> the great wonder of it all – that Christ would be glorified in us and God our Father would be praised.

We are sure to wilt a little along the way, but I hope you find encouragement in the next few paragraphs. I want joy for the journey, to build within your spirit. I want you to know without question that the waiting is worth it.

The waiting was worth it for my daughter Heaven whom I spoke of a few chapters ago. Remember she had been given a promise that she would receive a reward that would blow her mind. Our friend had come to a couple of track meets but when he had heard how successful she had been he was so impressed he went to work on her behalf. She had been a Justin Beiber fan and still is to tell the truth. She really wanted to attend his concert but it was sold out. Somehow, he was able to get her two tickets three rows from the front with a VIP meet and greet with Justin Beiber. She shrieked in excitement. She was overwhelmed with gratitude. He literally went far beyond what she could have imagined.

You might not want concert tickets. That was the desire of her heart but God knows what will make your heart swell with happiness. You have gotten this far, and you understand that complaining, having a poor attitude, and doubting can extend your waiting season, while obedience and full surrender to God can serve to maximize it. You know by now that there are things God scheduled for you that are only received through faith and patience. You accept that, although God has a good and perfect will for your life, His will for your life is not automatic. You have a part to play in activating and walking in that will. You realize there is a proving process in ***the space between.*** More importantly, you hold onto the truth that, like the diamond,

> you are designed to overcome. You are crafted to shine. You are coded to endure. You are slated to win. You are picked to prosper. You are selected to thrive.

Excuse me for a second while I remind you of who God says you are… just in case you doubt it at all. If even for a moment you looked in the mirror and a voice tried to rob you of your confidence, allow me to put you on notice. As a matter of fact, cut this out and place it on your mirror:

I am loved. Created in the image of God, I am treasured, brilliant, intelligent, and one of a kind. I am courageous, confident, and sure. I am called. I am destined to overcome, to persevere, to win, and to triumph. Goodness and mercy follow me; angels are assigned to me; and prosperity is my portion.

I am generous, obedient, and surrendered. I am built to last, to thrive, and to flourish. Good things come to me because I am righteous. I am favored. I am ahead and not behind, above and not below. I stand apart for I am set apart. I take pleasure in God's presence. I am His most treasured masterpiece, and nothing can defeat me, for I belong to God. My veins are filled with the history of champions. I am a descendant of the greats – Moses, Abraham, Deborah, Sarah, David, Joseph, Esther, Mary, and even our Lord Jesus Christ, who declared I am now a son/daughter of God. Therefore, I will not shrink back, step aside, walk with my head down, or stagger along the way. I will push forward and onward. Climb upward and over. Today and every day, I declare that I am not alone. Today I will win. I walk in health, and God has covered everything that concerns me because He cares for me. This is my confession.

Go Forth With Joy!

I want you to get this on the inside. You can do this! You can wait!

While you are waiting God is working.

You have what it takes to go through this season. One day you stand on the platform of your promise for all to see the brilliance of your life! You will glorify God for the work He has done. He is the wonder in the waiting, the greatest prize to obtain. He is:

Creator, Friend, Everlasting Father, Way Maker, Shield and Buckler, Protector, Healer, Companion, Love, Defender, Teacher, Redeemer, Savior, Restorer, Lover of our Souls, Champion, Provider, The Great I Am, The Author and Finisher of our Faith, King of all Kings, Promoter, He Who Sees ... He is God Almighty, The Lord Who Provides, The God Who Sees, Lord over all. There is none before Him nor will there be anyone

after Him. He has the final say and He says, even in this, He is able to cause you to triumph!

This is our God. He sits high above the heavens enthroned upon our hearts. He is the high and lofty One, the Rose of Sharon, and the still small voice. He makes our paths straight and adds light to our way. He elevates the humble and heals the sick.

God is able. He never fails. He never abandons.

He is an ever-present help in trouble. God holds us, keeps us, looks out for us, and blesses us.

God walks with us, counts every tear, feels every heartache, conquers every enemy, and helps us to recover. We can take the first step into faith holding His hand as He leads us to every good and perfect thing He has for us. Hold these words in your heart and remember God is always holding you in His.

See what kind of love the Father has given to us, that we should be called children of God; and so we are. 1 John 3:1, ESV

Know therefore that the LORD your God is God, the faithful God who keeps covenant and steadfast love with those who love him and keep his commandments, to a thousand generations. Deuteronomy 7:9, ESV

Through him we have also obtained access by faith into this grace in which we stand, and we rejoice in hope of the glory of God. More than that, we rejoice in our sufferings, knowing that suffering produces endurance, and endurance produces character, and character produces hope, and hope does not put us to shame, because God's love has been poured into our hearts through the Holy Spirit who has been given to us. Romans 5:2-5, ESV

Your steadfast love, O Lord, extends to the heavens, your faithfulness to the clouds.

Psalm 36:5, ESV

There is no desire of your heart that God does not know. There is no goal He is not equipped to help you achieve. God loves partnership. He wants to birth in your soul the dream He has prescribed just for you. He wants you to pursue Him with your whole heart. As you walk with Him, He will guide you through the testing seasons. He will guard you through the tempting moments and He will triumph through the times you feel torn apart. He is not a part time God. He is not a neglectful parent. He is fully invested in your future. He wants you and I to win.

Right now, as you are reading this, the hosts of Heaven are cheering you on. Jesus Christ your advocate is in Heaven praying on your behalf. The Holy Spirit is moving in your heart. You have everything you need to walk through this journey on the winning side. Don't back away from the tough decisions. So not shrink back from the sacrifice. Do not run from the difficult. Push through it one step at a time. One day at a time. One prayer at a time. Keep in your heart this truth,

God is with you.

You never wait alone and you never walk alone.

Practical Application

God is faithful. He will not delay. Never forget: No matter where you are on the journey, God is right there with you. Reach out and allow Him to love you and lead you all the way to seeing His promise fulfilled. Until then, enjoy the journey of the space between.

Consider It

As you look forward to the future, what are some decisions you have made about how you will wait on God?

___

___

___

___

___

You have an exciting future. What decisions have you made about your life after having read this book?

___

___

___

___

___

Write three things you now believe about God that you did not believe before reading this book:

1. ___

2. ___

3. ___

Internalize It

Meditate on and memorize this scripture:

Therefore, since we are surrounded by so great a cloud of witnesses, let us also lay aside every weight, and sin which clings so closely, and let us run with endurance the race that is set before us, looking to Jesus, the founder and perfecter of our faith, who for the joy that was set before him endured the cross, despising the shame, and is seated at the right hand of the throne of God. Hebrews 12:1-2, ESV

Speak It

"Jesus, how good You are! I am so excited to go on this adventure with You. I look forward to seeing what You reveal about Yourself as we go through seasons of waiting together. I am so thankful that You will make me more like You in the process! I decide today to throw off any of the weights that would hinder me from waiting well – weights like complaining, worry, fear, impatience –any weight that my try to delay your promise for me . Instead, I fix my eyes on You. I worship You. And I choose to be obedient and to enjoy Your holy presence while I wait."

Apply It

This is it – your moment of truth. Will you let the tools in this book change how you approach the in-between seasons?

Wait on the Lord; Be of good courage, And He shall strengthen your heart; Wait, I say, on the Lord! Psalm 27:14, NKJV

Here in this space, write today's date and the number one promise you are waiting on in your life. Set a reminder on your phone for a year from now. When it goes off, come back and write down what is happening with the promise and what you have learned in the meantime. Continue to do this until you see the promise come to pass. Then thank the Lord for all He has done in and through you during the process!

THE PROMISE:

Date:

ONE YEAR LATER:

TWO YEARS LATER:

THREE YEARS LATER:

The Call

If you have been walking this life tired of waiting, I want to invite you to rededicate your life to Jesus Christ who will never leave you in the space between. Maybe you don't have a relationship with God and He seems so far away. I extend to you the invitation to invite Him to be Lord of your life. My life truly changed once I changed controlling it. I want to pray with you as you say these words:

"God our Father, I come to you today in full surrender. I have not made the best choices and at times I have quit in the process. Today I choose to make the most important choice. I ask that you forgive my sins. I choose Jesus Christ as my Lord and my Savior. I believe in my heart You raised Him from the dead. I believe I am now born again and am now in the family of God."

If you said that prayer, I believe you are born again. I would love to celebrate this new decision with you. Let me know of your new commitment to Christ by emailing me at pastorsara.com